The Startup Masterplan

The Startup Masterplan

How to Build a Successful Business from Scratch

Nikhil Agarwal and Krishiv Agarwal

BEP

BUSINESS EXPERT PRESS

Leader in applied, concise business books

The Startup Masterplan: How to Build a Successful Business from Scratch

Cover design by Owais Ashraf

Interior design by Exeter Premedia Services Private Ltd., Chennai, India

First published in 2022 by
Business Expert Press, LLC
222 East 46th Street, New York, NY 10017
www.businessexpertpress.com

ISBN-13: 978-1-63742-202-1 (paperback)
ISBN-13: 978-1-63742-203-8 (e-book)

Business Expert Press Entrepreneurship and Small Business Management Collection

First edition: 2022

10 9 8 7 6 5 4 3 2 1

Description

Starting up is a game of choice rather than chance. 90 percent of startups fail in their first year! What are all of these firms doing wrong? How can I avoid such failures within my own ventures? It requires careful planning, expedient and rational decision making and lots of hard work. The payout is amazing, not only have you contributed to society massively but you've made a fortune for yourself and your family in the process. We can help you achieve this dream.

Using this book as a guide and a manual, you should be able to develop your entrepreneurial thinking skills, attain an overview on how to approach several essential aspects of starting up; from designing your brand to funding your venture. You will learn how to sustain your startup after it has finished the process of starting up because surviving in the cut-throat world of corporates is as hard as getting in there in the first place.

There's no need to reinvent the wheel to do the same mistakes which have been done before, it's better to learn from the specialist wisdom.

Learn it! Master it! Live by it!

Keywords

startups; venture funding; entrepreneurship; innovation; technology

Contents

Testimonials

"At the time of the global COVID-19 pandemic with its spillover impacts on the global economy, The Startup Masterplan *by Dr. Nikhil Agarwal and Krishiv Agarwal is coming at a moment when it's most needed. From the early stages of developing an idea and creating a business plan to generating funds through diversified sources, dealing with legal matters, and making decisions about future investments, this book offers a mindful recipe with step-by-step guide and practical advice on how to succeed as an entrepreneur. Written by the entrepreneurial guru Dr. Nikhil Agarwal with his outstanding experience and expertise in business development, technology, and innovation, along with the young entrepreneur Krishiv Agarwal, this book shares a sound formula of success that has the potential to create a new generation of entrepreneurs—the driving force of growth, creativity and innovation."* —**Dr. Esuna Dugarova, Policy Speciality, UNDP, New York**

The Startup Masterplan *provides crucial guidance to budding entrepreneurs, independent to region and industry. The core lessons that Dr. Nikhil Agarwal and Krishiv Agarwal offer to readers are the essential pieces needed when building a compelling business case coupled with an ambitious, yet achievable, company vision."* —**Ben Lakey, Royal Academy of Engineering Enterprise Fellow | CEO of Syndi Health, London**

"Nikhil Agarwal is one of those hidden gems who have done more to help entrepreneurs than most will ever realize. Not only has he helped (and nudged) those who were high-potential entrepreneurs, but he also has gently nudged those who weren't ready to do a rethink. Few people ever get credit for the latter, as important as it is. I met Nikhil via the erstwhile World Entrepreneurship Forum, and in a large room full of talented entrepreneur champions, he still stood out—one of those people you never want to lose track of. What I like about the book is its commonsense tone, more like someone recorded his conversations with present, past, and future entrepreneurs. Not much breathless, energized tome and even less pedantic academese. Are there spots where I want to argue with him? Of course. But don't you want a book

to inspire entrepreneurs to ask (and argue) the important questions with their mentors? In the United States, we often hear that any new venture needs a hacker, a hipster, and a hustler. You need a hacker to build and re-build till it works. You need a hipster to get in deep sync with your customers' thinking. You need a great hustler to energize the venture. Nikhil makes a good case that any of us can start being a hustler today, and we can grow into a great hustler, it just takes intelligent effort. How many promising ventures never happened because nobody saw themselves as having the right kind of "hustle?" I look forward to seeing how many discussions that Nikhil's new book will ignite."—**Professor Norris Krueger, Ex-External Fellow for the Max Planck Institute for Economics**

"Dr. Nikhil Agarwal and I are travelers. We have crossed many continents and countries exploring the application of technology in regard to its development. In many cases, we found that innovation emerges from below the radar and from the bottom-up perspective. We argued and conceptualised favoring the "street entrepreneurs" that daily reinvent themselves when "appropriating" technologies that weren't developed for poor or emerging countries. The outcome of our reflections by and large supports the idea that success happens when innovations transform the social landscape where they are fostered, empowering and equipping the very poor with new tools for intervention. This is what this book is about, an aid to support any entrepreneur."—**Dr. Luis Soares, University of Edinburgh, Edinburgh**

"My honest comment is—great job! Congrats! Few years ago, I was lucky to meet Nikhil. Not long after that, following him and his activities on a local and global level, I saw how professional and experienced he is. Knowing him and his results that are very visible and impactful, I can only say that this book is something special. So, dear readers, enjoy and grab everything that Krishiv and Nikhil shared with you."—**Jelena Plavanski, President, Serbia Angel Association, Belgrade**

Primer

Many people think that entrepreneurs are born, not made. Do not believe it! You do not have to be born with an entrepreneurial spirit to start a successful business. You can acquire the knowledge and skills to transform your idea from a thought to a business that provides a livelihood for you and your family. By taking a journey with us in this book, you can develop a mindset and skills to make your business idea a reality. You can learn the essential skills and ingredients to launch and sustain your business.

We'll start by exploring what it means to be an entrepreneur. It may surprise you! Then we'll help you refine and honestly evaluate your business idea. That can be hard work, but it will help separate your new business from those that fail. Starting a business, whether you are making a product or providing a service, can be scary. Anyone who tells you otherwise probably has never done it. We will work through how you can get comfortable with the idea of risk and then try to minimize those risks where possible. We'll help you figure out what is needed to make your business last long term and how to ensure that your business runs smoothly.

We want you to be able to look back with pride on your creation months and years from now. Many facets of decision making must explore and master to be as objective, critical, and correct as possible. Some valuable pointers toward better decision making include being objective, looking for facts, not settling for second best, looking for opportunities, and seeing the most beneficial.

One thing that is vitally important to your business is, naturally, the customer! While you may want to think that everyone will buy your product or service, you can't plan your business that way. It seems counterintuitive, but the truth is, if you try to sell to everyone, you will end up selling to no one.

Finally, we will help you plan for the future of your business. Remember, you aren't in this alone: we will brainstorm how you can find mentors, build your networking muscles, deal with failure, and plan your business without necessarily having a formal business plan.

Ready to ride the rocket ship that is being an entrepreneur? Strap yourself in!

PART I

Entrepreneurship is a difficult journey in which failure is commonplace. Although you cannot get rid of risks and bad luck, you can negate it with proper planning and sound decision making. The first part of this book will focus on the planning and setup for your business, and the second part will focus on decision making.

In planning, we will define entrepreneurship, explore an entrepreneurial genius's qualities of an entrepreneurial genius, and find the valid reasons to start a business. We will also explore the right time to start a business and the right place.

After that, we will study what makes or breaks a business, the business idea. We will test business ideas against questions and concerns until they are compatible with reality.

Then, we will take you down the road of converting your idea into a doable plan. We will teach you a few things along the way, such as doing market research, finding a good business name, critical thinking, and many more essential qualities of an entrepreneur and tools, to kickstart your business idea.

After making a business plan, we will explore sources for capital and find ways to legalize the business.

At the end of Part I, you will have all the tools ready to begin your business. Part II will help you in running it.

This book is not a one-time read, but more of something that you can refer to back and forth until you are comfortable with its contents.

The business world is ruthless, so good luck!

CHAPTER 1

Hustle Entrepreneur

Entrepreneurship is the backbone of a business. It is the brain; it is the masterplan. Our economies thrive in it, and technology is fueled by it. Entrepreneurship has to lead us into this exciting, high-tech reality in which we spend our lives. The entrepreneur is in the driving seat for humanity. The entrepreneur is an employer, a risk-taker, an innovator, and an investor. He (or she) brings riches to those who fund his (or her) expeditions and a source of income to those who work under him (or her). The entrepreneur is the golden boy of capitalism.

Business is the lifeblood of capitalism, and capitalism is the quintessence of our economies; our economies are the lifeblood of human civilization. Entrepreneurs are those who organize our factors of production, those who take risks in order to gain profit, which, in the end, benefit everyone through development and rising living standards. All in all, there are different and varied definitions of entrepreneurship, depending on whom you ask. There are some facts that are agreed by all those who define entrepreneurship, and these facts are:

1. Entrepreneurship involves creation or expansion of business.
2. It involves taking risks and accepting failure.
3. It requires talent to identify and exploits new opportunities to produce new products or to enter new markets.

The Entrepreneur

These myths and stories usually come in two forms. One story type is a tale of somebody who had an idea that very few understood or believed in, but the one with determination and perhaps sheer luck was in the right spot at the right time. A wonderful success story, with the two fundamentals of becoming a sucessful entrepreneur and some drama thrown in for good measure. Quite often, it is a story on a successful entrepreneur who has risen from rags to riches through hard work and an ability to make the right decisions at the right time. But the college dropout has not always been the entrepreneurial myth. We will explore some other models of the would-be entrepreneur.

For example, Hollywood has found great movie scripts in the entrepreneurial tales of the lives of Henry Ford and Thomas Alva Edison. Yet, Hollywood has yet to tell the stories of some famous female entrepreneurs like Madam C. J. Walker who turned her homemade recipes for hair and scalp care products into a business empire that made her the United States's first millionaire who was a self-made black woman in the early 1900s. The alternative story type is the story of a local or national entrepreneur celebrating an anniversary for being in business half a century and now handing over the firm to the next generation.

You are most likely to read these two types of stories because they are spectacular and entertaining. We may also be personally familiar with their products or services. You may even know these entrepreneurs personally. These stories are intriguing because they often capture the effect of *how dreams come true*, very proficiently. Have any of these entrepreneurs served as personal role models? Ask yourself whether reading any of these stories or seeing these movies made you dream that you could be an entrepreneur? Neither do you not have to be a dropout of a top college to have these dreams. Nor do you have to be under 60, or be independently wealthy to be an entrepreneur.

Entrepreneurial Dreams and Their Outcomes

Even Sigmund Freud would admit that both dreams and words can have various meanings. As with all words and dreams, they come with both good and bad connotations. The word *dream* is most likely related to the Germanic draugmus (meaning deception, illusion, or phantom) or the Norse draugr (ghost, apparition), or even the Sanskrit druh (seek to harm or injure).

Have you ever wondered whether your entrepreneurial dream could become one of these stories? Elias Howe (1819–1867) was reported to have said that the inspiration for his invention of the sewing machine came from a dream about being attacked by cannibals bearing spears that looked like the needle he then designed for his machine. Similarly Nikola Tesla is said to have been able to imagine a device in his mind's eye and then build it without ever having to write anything down, certainly an interesting form of *day dreaming*. Biographies of entrepreneurs who became self-made billionaires are frequently bestsellers much for the same reason. They tell stories of dreams coming true. One only needs to think of the recent biopic on Steve Jobs and the dramatic events at Apple or the movie *The Social Network* about Mark Zuckerberg and the drama behind the finding of Facebook.

We also see many of these stories focused on men, but one cannot ignore the stories of famous women entrepreneurs like Coco Chanel (fashion); or Madame C. J. Walker, Elizabeth Arden, Dame Anita Roddick, and Estée Lauder (cosmetics); or Olive Ann Beech (aircraft); Oprah Winfrey and Martha Stewart (media); or Ruth Handler (who gave us *Barbie* and co-founded Mattel Toys). How many of you are familiar with famous entrepreneurs from around the world who you most likely don't know that you know? Consider Sweden's Ingvar Kamprad (retail), or the Netherlands' Gerard Adriaan Heineken (brewing), or Chile's Don Melchor de Santiago Concha Toro and his wife Emiliana Subercaseaux (wineries), or Japan's Takeshi Mitarai (electronics).

In all these men and women, one can see a picture of the entrepreneur as a person who is visionary, hardworking, risk-taking, ambitious, having exceptional leadership skill, someone who never gives up, and a great source of inspiration. We like to describe them as having an entrepreneurial mindset.[1] What all these men and women have done is to show that these entreprenual qualities that they have, in combination with a brilliant idea and the ability to market, results in a firm that ultimately made the entrepreneur very wealthy. However, is wealth the only definition of success? For many of these people, success was changing an industry or creating something that was sustainable and enduring as a business over generations. To most of us, many of the companies cited are examples of successful entrepreneurs and entrepreneurship. They are enduring brands

---

[1] A.L. Carsrud and M. Brännback, eds. 2009. *Understanding the Entrepreneurial Mind: Opening the Black Box,* vol. 24. Springer Science and Business Media.

created centuries ago that we still use. Successful entrepreneurship is not only about what is created here and now. It is not only about computers and Internet business (Apple, Dell, Amazon, or eBay). It is also about sustainability over time. For a thorough discussion on lasting brands and their entrepreneurs, one needs to read Koehn (2001).[2]

There Is No One Narrative

The great engineer and scientist Nikola Tesla, who gave away many of his patents and was often a *loner*, is also a great example of someone using his own unique definition of success.

This is what we consider successful entrepreneurship and how we often describe a successful entrepreneur. Success is very much in the eye of the beholder and depends on the goals the entrepreneur has set for themselves. We have more to say about both the entrepreneurial mindset and success later in this book.

If you were to name a few successful entrepreneurs today, you are likely to mention Steve Jobs, Michael Dell, Martha Stewart, Mark Zuckerberg, Oprah Winfrey, and perhaps Henry Ford because you know or even own and use their products. Not all of you will know who Peter Thorwöste, Josiah Wedgwood, Erling Persson, Billy Durant, or Anita Roddick are. However, many of you know or own products from companies for whom these were the founders: FISKARS scissors, Wedgwood china, H&M clothing, General Motors, or the Body Shop cosmetics.

Consider Peter Thorwöste, who founded Fiskars Ironworks in 1649, which today is known as FISKARS, the global company manufacturing not just the scissors with the orange handles but also garden tools, ceramics, and boats. Fiskars is today a leading global supplier of branded consumer products for the home, garden, and outdoors. Brands like Fiskars, Iittala, Royal Copenhagen, Rörstrand, Arabia, Buster, and Gerber all belong to the Fiskars brand palette.

So is Heinz, today most well-known for its ketchup. Few of us may know that their breakthrough product was pickled horseradish.

---

[2] N.F. Koehn. 2001. *Brand New: How Entrepreneurs Earned Consumers' Trust from Wedgwood to Dell.*

Their well-known logo *57 Varieties* was created in 1896, and was the first electric sign on Manhattan lit in 1900. Recently, H. J. Heinz has been purchased from the founding family by Warren Buffett's Berkshire Hathaway and 3G Capital. Then there is the Henry Ford and the Ford Motor Company that changed not only manufacturing processes but also the automotive industry.

On the newer side, we have seen the rise of tech giants such as Google and Amazon. They have found success selling products on the new frontier of business: the Internet. Google's case is fascinating because a lot of its revenue comes from advertising. Google's search engine is known for its incredible accuracy in predicting what the consumer wants, to such a degree that some would say, "It knows what you are going to buy before you even want it." While their other platform for advertising, YouTube is often blamed for its inconsistent advertising policies. What can spell success in one market does not mean the same thing in another.

Google's Failure in Advertising With YouTube

Google has not had the expected success for advertising on YouTube. They have had many problems with advertising, mainly with finding the right content to place advertisements on it. The problem with that strategy contradicts Google's search engine advertising strategy, which places ads on content based on the user rather than the content. If Google could personalize ads to users than content creators, then Google could save millions in legal fees for disputes on unfair judgment on lack of monetization of content and billions in lost revenue. On the other hand, Facebook has a very profitable advertising system, even though they have a distribution of very similar content.

Collective Dreams

We all dream. Dreams are a part of many inventions. If we think of technology, then Thomas A. Edison often comes to mind. He was an *inventor* and entrepreneur who brought electric lights into homes and founded electric generation companies that still bear his name, even General Electric (GE) was founded by Edison. However, the story of electricity would not be complete without acknowledging Nikola Tesla who many say was the first to develop alternating current (among many other numerous breakthrough inventions) while Edison's team focused on direct current.

As with all breakthrough inventions, many people are involved. For example, there were 22 others ahead of Edison in inventing the light bulb, but it was Edison who knew the power of marketing and branding. That is, pioneers in an industry like Tesla are often not the ones who win the prize or the wealth and acclaim, but those who came after them and understood how to develop a business model to exploit that invention. Success is not always about being first, or as some say, one gets "shot by other pioneers coming up behind you." Part of the task of any entrepreneur is to get those on their teams to have similar dreams, if not buy into the one of the founder(s).

Tesla Versus Edison

Nikola Tesla and Thomas Edison were pioneers of their time but sworn rivals too. From the light bulb and the Telsa tower to alternating and direct current, Edison and Tesla always had their disputes. Even though Tesla was ahead of his time, inventing wireless electricity and X-rays, his entrepreneurial adventures failed, and he died an impoverished man. On the other hand, Edison was not even the inventor of the light bulb, just the guy who popularized it. This was not because of his scientific genius but his entrepreneurial one. Unlike Tesla, he was focused on making his idea a successful business, not just a dream for the future. Although he was successful in his circumstance and in his way, ahead of his time, business-wise, he was not.

Make products like Tesla, but think and sell like Edison.

Why Entrepreneurship Became Important

Here we are going to get a bit academic, so forgive us. You should realize that the terms entrepreneurship and entrepreneur have been around for centuries. Some consider Cantillion in 1755 as having been the first to mention the phenomena in a published work. Still others claim Say (1803) was the first. Regardless, Hoselitz (1951) finds early traces in historical dictionaries to the Middle Ages in the normal course of development of the French language. The most general and probably the earliest meaning is "celui qui entreprend quelque chose," which literarily means "he who gets things done," in other words an active person. The preceding discussion shows that the term has stirred up considerable academic debate for quite some time, even though Schumpeter (1934) is often considered to be the intellectual father of the modern field of entrepreneurship.

It is our considered opinion that entrepreneurship became important in contemporary life in 1987 to be precise, in that year, entrepreneurship came to be regarded as a significant factor in national wealth creation, not just personal wealth creation. It, thus, entered the awareness of the wider, modern, audience. In 1987, David Birch published his book *Job Creation in America*. This book resulted from a longitudinal study at the Massachusetts Institute of Technology (MIT) between 1969 and 1986. The study traced 12 million individual business establishments during this period. The raw data was Dun and Bradstreet (D&B), single-unit standalone companies, a store, a small plant, or a law firm. In 1986, the establishments employed 95 percent of all non-governmental workers in the United States. The complete files of D&B were tapped regularly during this period. The files had information on employment rolls, age, and location of each establishment.

Birch's study showed that small startup firms were responsible for more than 80 percent of all new jobs created in the United States, and that large corporations decreased employment. Small firms are more likely to expand than large organizations. Suppose large firms were to create new jobs that would take place through a new business unit, not a new firm. To be blunt: large firms create new jobs through the formation of new business units. Mom and Pop Delis open up a second store managed by the owner's daughter. Statistics from the U.S. Small Business Administration have, over the years, remained reasonably stable, and the same holds for most Western countries; 99.5 percent of all firms in a country are classified as small firms. This holds for the United States, Australia, Chile, India, or Finland. In 2015, there is evidence from the United States that 310 new entrepreneurs per 100,000 adults were added each month. This is up from a monthly average of 280 in 2014. The data indicates entrepreneurial levels have returned to a more normal pattern since the Great Recession of 2008, of equal interest, is that in 2013, 23 million people were self-employed. For whatever reason, more and more individuals are choosing different paths to be an entrepreneur.

Chapter Summary

Entrepreneurship is a skill that involves learning how to create or expand businesses, take risks, look for the right opportunities, make rational decisions in highly high-pressure situations, be a great leader, and think long term.

- There are stereotypical stories of great entrepreneurs, which usually fall into two categories, the rags to riches college dropout who came up with a brilliant idea and became a tycoon because of his or her doing. Then, the established heir gets a decently sized business but expands it greatly and takes it to new heights. You have to be neither to be a successful entrepreneur, and this is important to remember.
- Business is about long-term sustainability, and the money is not only in what is popular right now. In order to find success, you must look through a different lens—a lens of an opportunist, of a visionary, and of someone who looks for problems and potential solutions.
- What works in one industry or one company may not work in another. You should always look at what is working and try and create your solutions. Idealism is irrelevant; it does not matter how efficient, effective, or pleasant something is on paper; when it comes to creating lasting and sound systems, the real-life results matter more than anything else.
- Startups and entrepreneurs are the backbones of the economy. Without them, there is no improvement, no production, no growth. Despite public opinion, most entrepreneurs and business people work extremely hard for high pay, but their jobs require an intense focus, deep knowledge in multiple fields, pristine social skills, and the ability to handle high amounts of stress and are willing to work any given time when necessary.

CHAPTER 2

The Process of Starting Up

A startup is not just a newborn company but rather a means to balance in a market. Startups are essential for the healthy functioning of an economy, in a capitalistic one at least. They dream of gaining unfathomable riches with the reality of hard work and contribution to society. Without startups, innovation would not exist, and competition would be a long-forgotten thing. In order to progress humanity, startups are a must. So startup, get set, and go!

> *Deciding on an idea for business consists of seeing what everybody else has seen and thinking what nobody else has thought.*
>
> —Albert von Szent-Györgyi

> *Be original … unless you want to get very rich, very fast—then copy like crazy.*
>
> —Dan S. Kennedy

Not long ago, a medical researcher in London spent an afternoon visiting an art gallery. One of the more intriguing displays he saw used magnets to move colored metal particles inside glass tubes. Another display used the repelling force of a giant magnet to levitate a series of smaller magnets. Sometime later, he inexplicably thought of these exhibits, which led him to the belief that it just might be possible to use magnets to push and pull ionized cancer medications directly into tumors. As a result, a new field of medicine was born.

Just as with science, the business also can merge what may appear to be two seemingly unrelated fields that lead to something completely new. Note, however, that the researcher in the preceding example would not have come up with his groundbreaking idea if he had not first discovered a field of interest that excited him and if he had declined to take an interest in the world around him. It is not much different for those wishing to start a new business. Prospective entrepreneurs should start with an interest or passion in a field, area, or product and explore the purpose and goals behind why they want to make a significant change in their life. This type of honesty and insight often prove invaluable in ensuring that the rationale behind a proposed business is valid.

Starting a New Business

Popular opinion suggests that owning a business involves working flexible hours, not being beholden to anyone, having the ability to make independent decisions, and, in effect, being entirely on one's own. Equally as ubiquitous is the belief that because life has not quite turned out the way it was envisioned, entrepreneurship is as good an instigator of change as any to chart a new course to success. Unfortunately, in both these cases, reality can be quite different from what is believed.

What is needed to be successful in business? According to experienced entrepreneurs, apart from a sound idea and a combination of good reasons, one must desire to set out into the unknown with the heart of an explorer and the mind of a business contractor. In addition, it must be understood that a journey laden with risk, hard work, sacrifice, and occasional setbacks is what lies ahead.

If this sounds somewhat harsh, consider that in some cases, up to 90 percent of new enterprises go out of business within the first three to five years of operation. Traditionally, it was usually assumed that many startups go bust due to a lack of research and preparation, poor business practices, or unforeseen economic influences. Nevertheless, a growing number of researchers think that a large number of businesses *fail* because their overworked owners decided that the rewards are not worth the effort, so the plug is deliberately pulled.

Entrepreneurial Genius

Key message: Genius is a trick of mind.

Tea bags, liquid soap, and highlighter pens, the world is full of good, commercially viable ideas that seem obvious now but did not exist until someone thought of them. How did they do it?

Deciding on an idea for business can be difficult. The world is a crowded marketplace. There are two ways of generating new ideas. One is to wait for inspiration to strike. It may work, but it is uncertain. This chapter explains how to coax ideas by applying a little genius. Emphatically, entrepreneurial genius does not require sophisticated scientific or technical knowledge. Genius resides in how we think about things. The BlackBerry mobile phone has captured a market lead in e-mail that rivals have struggled to beat. The device is packed full of complicated electronics, but its success rests as much as anything on a shift in thinking. Hitherto, handheld e-mail devices had relied upon the concept of *pull*, requiring users to expend time in opening up their e-mails. By contrast, the attraction of the BlackBerry is that it is based on the opposite concept of *pushing* e-mails out to recipients. Clever research and development scientists worked hard to make *pull* e-mail devices better, faster, user-friendly, and so forth. Yet so long as their thinking was constrained within the parameters of the *pull* concept, they were limited in what they could achieve.

Most genius comes from thinking outside the box. Elon Musk, the founder of SpaceX, Tesla, and many other companies, is known for this. He founded eBay too, which revolutionized online shopping that has become the household name. SpaceX is a space firm that currently has the objective of getting humans to Mars.

Genius is a trick of mind that can be learned. The trick resides in questioning the obvious, in questioning received ways of doing things

---

SpaceX

When Elon Musk decided that he would start SpaceX, he figured he would need rockets to launch cargo into space. The problem was that all space rockets were government-made, and the rest were for a nuclear detonation. So, with out-of-the-box thinking and many long nights, he came up with his in-house rocket. Any other investor or entrepreneur would have missed this billion—possibly trillion-dollar opportunity, but with Elon's application of critical and out-of-the-box thinking, he was able to make SpaceX the company it is today.

and demolishing concepts that are blocking progress. Incidentally, even if you already have an idea for business or are already in business, you may still find what follows useful.

It is necessary to have the entrepreneurial genius to run a startup. Without genius, it is very likely to fail.

Becoming a Genius

Blocking assumptions are everywhere. They frequently reside in *taken-for-granted* assumptions and practices. For example, when we say *pen*, we almost invariably think *ink*. It is obvious, is it not? The trouble is, if we never looked beyond the obvious, we would never have invented the electronic pen we use to sign for parcel deliveries. The aeroplane is modeled on the concept of a bird. It has wings. We can improve the wings by streamlining, but in order to invent the helicopter, we needed to demolish the assumption that flying machines need wings. Shoes may have laces, but that doesn't mean that they need them. Early train carriages had compartments because they were based on the concept of horse and carriage. Open-plan seating made carriages cheaper to haul because they were lighter and accommodated more passengers, but they were only invented by dropping the original concept.

We sometimes make assumptions without realizing them. Before Allen Lane, books were expensive partly because they had cardboard covers. Lane made business history (and a fortune) by reinventing the *book* as a paperback. Wind farms are unpopular. Critics argue that the amount of electricity generated does not justify their unsightly appearance in the rural landscape. There seems to be no easy answer if we assume that windmills need to stand on land, that is. In fact, trials are afoot to float them at sea.

What is a mobile phone these days? It might be a camera, or an MP3 player, or an organizer. It may also send and receive telephone calls and text messages. Once we drop the original concept of *telephone* and redefine it, say, as a miniature computer, we can glimpse other possibilities. It is a question that is exercising the banking industry because technological innovations will soon enable us to operate a bank account from a mobile phone. Once the technology is in place, there may be little to stop mobile phone companies from offering banking services.

How we conceptualize something determines what we see and how we see. If I say the word *time*, you will probably immediately think *clock*. Yet, a clock is just a human invention to help us understand the notion of *time*. Without clocks to regulate time, life as we know it would break down. Trains could not run *on time* (not that they do anyway); the conference call could not take place at 8 o'clock in the morning if we did not all measure time in the same way. Yet, useful though the concept is, it also constrains our thinking. We think of time as something that passes, but where does it go to after it passes? We think of the past as irretrievable, yet some things happen time and time again. More importantly, the clock moves forward. Stephen Hawking's genius lay in realizing that physicist had unconsciously restricted their thinking by always imagining time as moving forward. Hawking did something simple but profound. He imagined time as moving backward as well as forward. This insight enabled physicists to conceptualize the notion of stars collapsing backward as they were sucked into black holes.

Entrepreneurs too can glimpse new possibilities by ridding themselves of blocking assumptions. If we assume soap always comes in blocks, we will never be able to imagine it in liquid form. If we confine our thinking about chips to potatoes, we will never imagine the possibility of parsnip and beetroot chips. Likewise, when we think *lock*, we may automatically imagine *key*. Locks may have keys, but we have invented many different kinds of *key*, such as electronic cards. Many cities have broken the blocking assumption that big events such as football matches take place inside a stadium by opening up free space and exploiting the possibilities of wide-screen television.

Good Reasons for Thinking About Starting a Business

Because starting up a business can be difficult, it is a good idea for a beginner to have several good reasons as to why he or she would like to become an entrepreneur. The most common of these are:

- A desire to be one's boss and handle more responsibility
- A love of complex challenges
- The seeking of career independence as well as more control over life and its direction

- A significant *life change* has occurred (i.e., divorce, disability, job loss, pregnancy, retirement)
- The entrepreneur has invented, developed, or innovated a new product or service
- A current job is going nowhere
- Money has suddenly become available (i.e., an inheritance, the lottery, asset selling)
- An opportunity has made itself known (i.e., a local business is up for sale; a group of people whose needs are not being met has been spotted, or a product people would pay for has been discovered)

Wrong Reasons for Starting a Business

Starting a business with the wrong motivation or reason can lead to the downfall of a good business, and if proper care is not taken, it could affect an entrepreneur for a long time. Some experienced entrepreneurs have identified some poor motivators for starting a business, and they will be discussed as follows:

- **Desperation**. Make no mistake; desperation is a powerful motivational stimulus. However, it can also lead to poor judgment, rash decisions, and a dangerous leap into untested waters.
- **There is nothing else to do**. Feeling that no other options are available shows a lack of commitment and passion—two essential elements compromise successful entrepreneurship.
- **There is lots of money to be made**. This is a pipe dream, and it is often fueled by media stories that highlight app/software developers (or others) who struck it rich *overnight*. However, entrepreneurs must be realistic with their expectations and know the difference between making a one-time-only profit, making a living, and daydreaming. The vast majority of successful entrepreneurs make a living, not a fortune.
- **Owning a business will make life easier**. Unfortunately, having a business usually increases one's responsibilities. That does not translate into making life easier.

- **The entrepreneur cannot work with others**. Suppose a wannabe entrepreneur cannot work with other people. In that case, he or she is going to have countless problems dealing with customers, bankers, a landlord, suppliers, local or federal agencies, a parent company (if the entrepreneur is involved in a franchise), and the many other people who are often both directly and indirectly involved in private enterprise.
- **Owning a business will provide more free time**. Running a business is time-consuming and life-consuming. Every entrepreneur who has ever shared their experience stated that they worked longer and harder running their own business than they ever did working for someone else.

Do You Have What It Takes?

Having talked about becoming a genius and why not, it is only plausible to ask if one has what it takes to own a business and become successful. One can be a genius but not have the right emotional intelligence and the proper discipline to put things in place for business. Lots of businesses have failed because the owner does not have the right work ethic. Therefore, emphasis will be laid on what it takes in this part of the book.

As President John F. Kennedy once said, we do not choose to go to the moon because it is easy—we go because it is hard. So it is with entrepreneurship. Starting (and running) a commercial enterprise requires developing new skills, seizing the initiative, rising while others sleep, working evenings and weekends and holidays, and taking educated risks. In addition, unique and sometimes conflicting qualities and character traits—often considered inappropriate in refined social settings—are also required, such as a rabid hatred of losing and a bit of obsessive behavior. Simply put, being goal-oriented and having a bit of business talent are not enough on their own because, as the saying goes, talent without discipline is like an octopus on roller-skates. Knowing how to apply your strengths, weaknesses, and differences in an appropriate context is also crucial as is having the guts to do things never before attempted, even though you are a bit reticent or afraid. The bottom line is that most business success is not dependent on luck—unless luck is defined as preparation meeting opportunity (according to some surveys, succeeding as an entrepreneur often means toiling 65 to 85 hours a week or more). But first things first. Whether you want to start an enterprise from scratch or try something new in an existing organization, before the hard work and risk-taking commence, you must first be ready and willing to face the unknown with the best that humanity has to offer—the human spirit. If you do not fire yourself up and use your enthusiasm to make thorough preparations, there is a good chance that your proposed business project will be sunk before it begins. The following sections reveal many of the qualities and attributes that successful entrepreneurs often possess but paradoxically do not always need to have.

Stage I: The Right Attitude

Every endeavor, large or small, benefits from a proper mindset. As Henry Ford once said, whether you believe you can or believe you cannot, you are right. In the business world, this means having or developing above-average levels of the following before beginning a business endeavor:

- Drive and determination: Including initiative, high energy levels, and a hearty appetite for achievement.
- Ambition: Harboring a fierce desire to succeed and forming a substantial, realistic, and personal definition of exactly what success is.
- Intelligence: The desire and aptitude to gather, interpret, and prioritize information.
- Commercial intellect: The motivation and know-how to scan business environments for weaknesses, threats, and opportunities.
- Confidence: The courage to be decisive and assured (not arrogant), with your abilities.
- Curiosity: An innate interest in the world and how it works.
- The will to win: The determination to come out on top rather than just participate. (For example, consider the thousands of entrants that enter big city marathons. Only a dozen or so can expect to win. Most are happy to finish the course. In business, you must enter to win.)

Stage II: Implementation (Putting Plans Into Action)

Winning as an entrepreneur is based on being a doer, not a dreamer. This means having the guts to leave the comfort of familiar surroundings and march off into the unknown with a well-honed idea and a keen sense of adventure. Prerequisites for these attributes include:

- Communication skills: The aptitude to state what is needed clearly and concisely.
- Motivation: A willingness to work long hours whether you feel like it or not.
- Self-discipline: The ability to rein in temptation or excess.
- Persuasiveness: The ability to convince others and inspire them to do your bidding.
- Speed and agility: The ability to respond intelligently to situations both rapidly and effectively.

Stage III: Diligence (Going the Distance)

Developing the fortitude and determination to stay on track is probably the most difficult of all entrepreneurial abilities. Launching and running a business is time-consuming, life-consuming, and full of distractions and setbacks. Surviving the process with grace requires:

- Resilience: The capacity to learn from mistakes, brush off adversity, and pull yourself together after suffering through the inevitable losses that running a business involves.
- Perseverance: Steadfastness and consistency (not stubbornness) with goals.
- Humility: Maintaining a genuine conviction to serve others.
- Reliability: Being responsible, accountable, and available.
- Temperament: Keeping a sense of calm, balance, and proportion, no matter what happens.
- Endurance: The ability to bear the ups and downs of a working day with patience and fortitude and come back for more.

- Flexibility: Greeting the forces of change and being willing to adapt.
- Understanding: Accepting that people are different and being able to empathize with them.

What is the Right Time to Start a New Business

Many business enthusiasts have claimed that now is a better time to own a business and run a business. However, new and aspiring entrepreneurs must do their research, take notes, and be sure to pinpoint what they want to achieve before they start. It is also vital for potential entrepreneurs to examine what it means to own a business. Additionally, potential entrepreneurs have to understand the process of owning a business and how it will be addressed. Without this knowledge (which can take six months or longer to accumulate), the entrepreneur will probably not be ready for business ownership. Just as important, critical outside obligations (e.g., the onset of medical treatment, college tuition payments, financial problems, unresolved crisis, personal dilemmas, and so on) should be taken care of beforehand to avoid distractions. The understanding and support of partners, spouses, or children is equally crucial because many experienced practitioners insist that entrepreneurs do not have much time to spend with their loved ones during the first few years of a new business venture.

What about the economy? Is it prudent to wait for the economy to improve before starting a business? Disney, Hewlett-Packard, and Microsoft all started during economic downturns—as did half of the 30 companies that comprise the Dow Jones Industrial Average. Indeed, some analysts claim that a recession is a great time to open a business because wages are down, rents are cheaper, competition is scarce, and goods and services can be found at a discount. That being said, there is no definitive proof to suggest that recessions make starting a business easier. The availability of resources, personal abilities, and the current circumstances of the entrepreneur should all play significant roles in determining the best time to start up a business.

Where Should You Start a Business?

To give an obvious answer to this question, it will be "where there are plenty of customers for your product or services." However, the potential entrepreneur must consider the details of the area where these potential customers are located. If, by chance, you find yourself liking a place while away on vacation, and you feel you will get many customers there if you start a business, the next thing to do is to make sure you make your research and findings of the place.

According to the World Bank's International Finance Corporation (IFC), entrepreneurs planning on starting a business in a foreign country or unfamiliar area should first ensure that the following situations exist:

1. There should be a low number of rules, regulations, paperwork, and licenses so that the business and its activities can be made legitimate promptly.
2. The business owner should be able to hire and fire employees with relative ease.
3. The business owner should have the capacity to draw up and enforce a legal contract.
4. The business owner should be able to obtain credit or borrow money.
5. A low number of steps and procedures should exist so that the business can either be closed down—or bankruptcy can be declared—with relative ease.

Advice From Professionals

The answer to why, when, and where a business should be situated makes up the foundation of a successful business startup. If there is a nagging interest in you to start a business, many answers will begin to fall in place for your questions as you begin to research yourself and your reasons for wanting a business. This was stated by a restaurant owner, Bernard Marche, the founder of the *Chick-a-Chick* café in Warsaw, Poland. To nullify any form of surprises and the expenses that come with them, it is crucial to examine every economic, environmental, and financial situation surrounding you before you kick yourself into action. Some additional advice from professionals who have been successful in their dealings as an entrepreneur are further listed as follows:

- Make sure you do not jump or rush into uncharted territory. What this means is, do not leap before looking. Instead, look before you leap.

- Know the unexpected places where an entrepreneurial lifestyle may lead. For example, if you are a jewelry worker who loves the craft, but you are sick and tired of laboring for someone else and want to spend more time working as a designer, bear in mind that running your own business may involve more administrative than creative work.
- Yes, it is possible to bake cookies, or build a piece of furniture, or design a website for a friend and be paid for it. However, if you want to turn these pastimes into a business, you must first find out if producing them regularly can secure a living. Is there an ongoing market for these products/services in your area? If not, can you afford to attract distant customers and ship your product to them? Will the money you generate be enough to pay a mortgage and bills and support your family?
- Before you venture into an entrepreneurial journey, make sure you prepare your mind ahead for the possible obstacles that may come your way. It is sporadic to experience novel situations in businesses. Therefore, it is possible to figure out what lies ahead if you take your time to study every situation surrounding you.
- Do not leave a paying job to start your enterprise until you have first sorted out what you want to do, the direction you want to go, and the best time to start. Keep your current job while examining the self-employment options available. That way, you will not be deprived of income before you begin.
- If your idea is rock solid and carried out all your research, start immediately and with prudence. Guide against the number one killer in the business world, *procrastination*.
- Whether starting a business or launching a new product, remember that the idea is to score goals, not just kick the ball. A 100 percent commitment is mandatory. The harder you work, the luckier you get. As famed Hollywood film producer Mike Todd once said, the meek may inherit the earth, but not in our lifetime.
- Lastly, consider the often told (probably apocryphal) story about two explorers that a shoe company sent to a primitive

part of the world to determine the market's viability. "Complete disaster!" wired the first explorer, "No one here wears shoes." The telegram from the second explorer arrived a few hours later. "Fantastic opportunity!" it read, "No one here wears shoes!"

Ten Keys to Innovation

The only way you can start a business is with an idea. This will help.

The best way to coax ideas is to be systematic. Imagine that what follows is like a bunch of keys. Work through them one by one. Some may not be helpful, but others may unlock entrepreneurial potential.

Key 1: Reinvent the Familiar

While it is wise to learn from experience, it is wiser to learn from the experience of others.

—Rick Warren

One approach to inventing new ideas involves taking familiar products or services for which there is already a market and reinventing them. Take the aforementioned humble potato chips. When I was a child, the only varieties on offer were *plain* and *cheese and onion*. There followed a flood of innovations. Likewise, the laptop computer introduced portability into a world dominated by desktop machines. Social entrepreneurs in the 19th and early 20th centuries who established the cooperative stores, and even pubs as cooperatives, were not anti-profit but challenged the idea of private appropriation. Boutique hotels offer guests services plus a personal touch that reduces the anonymity and loneliness of large hotels in large cities. In order to see new possibilities, try questioning basic concepts and assumptions. What is a hotel? Is it a sleeping factory or a place where guests come to enjoy good food and relax in pleasant and secure surroundings? Ask silly questions. The answers may be very rewarding.

Asking obvious (silly) questions can be extremely rewarding. For instance, why do guests need hotels? Wouldn't they rather be at home? These seemingly silly questions were the precursor to the development of timeshare apartments in cities such as London catering for the more affluent visitors where guests' personal effects are stored and laid in anticipation of visits to create a feeling of being *at home*. At the other end of the socio-economic scale, housing associations have made homes affordable by breaking the conventional assumption that ownership means that one must own a whole house. Instead, associations retain partial ownership and offer buyers the opportunity to acquire a percentage of the equity, thus enabling people who might otherwise be left behind to secure a toehold on the property ladder.

Another excellent example of this is electric cars. When Elon Musk decided that he would dedicate his life to clean energy, space exploration, and the Internet, he thought about implementing the clean energy part. Thinking about that led him to create Tesla, an electric car company that is now a household name worldwide. He reinvented the familiar cars and added a game-changing feature, electricity. Although his idea was met with problems, he and his team solved them and made handsome profits in return.

Asking these questions and thinking from multiple perspectives is a crucial skill for an entrepreneur. You must look out for these questions because they help you determine the validity of a business idea and sometimes even help you forge new ones.

Key 2: Improve the Familiar

Without change, there is no innovation, no creativity, or incentive for improvement.

—William Pollard

Innovation is creating something new. The most productive way to do this is to improve what is already there. Not only are present technologies readily acceptable and deployable because they are already in use and present in the market, but they are also cheaper to develop upon as you do not have to start from scratch. The brainstorming part is more straightforward, too; all you have to do is scrutinize and figure out the problems in an existing product and improve upon them.

In the 19th century, an entrepreneur named George Mortimer Pullman built opulent railway carriages and introduced innovations such as onboard catering and *at seat* services in return for a supplement. Mortimer took ordinary train travel and made it better. The idea sold in developed countries all over the world and lives on in tours like the Orient Express.

Entrepreneurially minded farmers have also seen possibilities in organic meat and vegetables. They succeed by offering what supermarkets struggle to imitate, such as rare varieties, unusual recipes, exceptionally well-hung meats, and so forth. Dyson vacuum cleaners are vacuum cleaners made better. Videoconferencing saves time, money, and effort and helps to protect the environment. Yet it is not used as much as it could be because the equipment is cumbersome and temperamental. In year 2020–2021, due to the COVID-19 situation, Zoom grabbed the world market for easy videoconferencing using the Internet. Tiptree would have been lost if they had challenged the big companies directly. Instead, they made jam and marmalade with a substantially greater proportion of fruit to sugar than the big manufacturers saw fit to offer and also offered a much wider range of flavors, such as ginger and pineapple, in contrast to the more familiar strawberry and raspberry. Tiptree has since extended their approach to ketchups and chutneys.

A fallacy arises while doing, in which the entrepreneur thinks that they have developed a completely new product just by changing one or two features about it. The problem with that is that if the changes are easily replicable, then established companies will easily copy your idea and make money off it while your business crumbles. Always be sure you have enough changes made, and they are substantial, something unique that other companies could not easily replicate.

Key 3: Reduce Loss

One way of improving a product or a service is to reduce the loss that it imparts to a customer. The following are some examples of loss:

- Queuing at a hotel checkout
- Waiting for a computer to *boot up*
- The background *hiss* the television makes
- Clothes that need washing
- Window frames that need painting

- Cars that need servicing
- The weight of a lawnmower
- Waiting in a doctor's surgery
- Preparing a supermarket in readiness for customers
- The time it takes to microwave a meal

Loss refers to anything that imparts cost but no value. For instance, queuing at a hotel checkout means guests lose time. Some hotels employ extra staff at peak times to reduce the loss. (A surprising number don't.)

Better still, some operate express checkouts where departing customers receive their bills under their doors during the night and report to checkout only if the bill is incorrect. All else being equal, where would you rather stay? And would you rather hump a heavy lawnmower over the grass or use one that floats over the surface? We can invent better soap powders and detergents, but what customers really want is clean clothes.

Tesco's decision to move to 24-hour opening was partly driven by the sheer cost of activities associated with opening up and shutting down stores in the morning and at night. A famous example of reducing loss to the customer is the Dyson vacuum cleaner, which dispensed with the additional expense of buying dust bags. A more recent innovation that also reduces loss to the customer has been to abandon the traditional *four-wheel* and mount the machine on a ball to improve efficiency and handling.

Just as in real life, losses are an inconvenience. When purchasing a product or opting for a service, it is a superb idea to analyze each opportunity from a loss perspective rather than a benefit one because the losses are usually of time, which tends to be overlooked.

An excellent example of this is an case of opportunity cost. Jared runs a medical store. He earns 100 dollars an hour from selling medicine. He gets an offer to supply medicine to a large hospital at the rate of 75 dollars an hour. Should he take the job? No. He should not. He would be losing 25 dollars an hour. It is an apparent loss, but at first glance, one might think that he is gaining money from accepting the offer. That is why you must analyze in terms of loss. The right question is never, "what will I gain?"; it is always, "What will I lose?"

Key 4: Solve Problems

Life is full of people waiting to be discovered! I once stayed in a friend's house. I boiled an egg for breakfast and then realized that the house was devoid of eggcups. Only by trying to eat an egg off a plate did I realize how useful an eggcup is. Who invented it? Fountain pens that ran out of ink were a nuisance until someone invented cartridges. We never thought much about how messy and restricting wires are until Bluetooth technology arrived.

In order to solve problems, you have to recognize their existence and then ask yourself what you can do about it. That means being willing to challenge the status quo and *taken-for-granted* assumptions about what is acceptable and what can be changed. It means thinking about what *could be* as distinct from what merely *is*. It is the difference between asking *why* and *why not*, Chad Varah, who founded the Samaritans in the early 1950s, noted that on average, three people committed suicide every day in London. Was this an acceptable state of affairs? Was there nothing he could do?

Chad Varah's starting point was to challenge the assumption that crisis counseling is necessarily a specialized task. His starting point was to assert that ordinary men and women with training in only a few basic principles could be effective and then to mobilize that potentially immensely powerful resource. More recently, some entrepreneurially minded companies thought seriously about the implications of diminishing reserves of oil and began to develop hybrid petrol/electric cars. The prototypes were frequently the butt of jokes, but people are no longer laughing.

Key 5: Take What Nobody Wants

"Where there's muck, there's brass." As this homely Northern saying recognizes, fortunes have been built by entrepreneurs focusing upon what no one else wants and not just hawking manure either!

The philosophical starting point rests in the notion of the empty. Try pouring coffee into a full cup. It will spill over and make a mess because the cup is already full. So, the cup is most beneficial when it is empty. Large, established businesses are likewise *full*. They are full of products, full of commitments. Entrepreneurial potential resides not in competing for head-on with giants but in exploring the empty space, the things that large organizations are not interested in.

The post office geared itself to receive pennies and has pennies saved by the thrifty poor customers for whom the grand Victorian banks did not cater. The low-cost airline easyJet was launched from regional airports that the big airlines shunned, where landing fees were correspondingly cheap. The Naxos record company focused on older works that were out of copyright, and relatively unknown artists. (There is also a lesson for career building here as many of those artists are now well known.)

Key 6: Make the Expensive Cheap

It is almost a cliché to cite Henry Ford's Model T car as an example of opening up an expensive entity to mass production. Happily, there are other examples in business history. The uniformly priced postage stamp facilitated mass communications. In the 1950s, Berni Inns made eating in restaurants possible for lower-income citizens. More recently, *pay as you go* services have made mobile phones universally affordable.

In school and higher education, the emphasis is upon adding to knowledge. By contrast, entrepreneurs subtract. Rowland Hill, who is credited with the invention of the postage stamp, got rid of a system of complicated tariffs based on weight and distance, and introduced a single uniform charge encapsulated in the stamp known as the *Penny Black*. Berni Inns reduced the price of meals by removing tablecloths, thereby saving over 250,000 dollars a year in laundry, and substituting table mats; by reducing the number of dishes on offer to cut the cost of inventory; and by keeping dishes simple so that they could be cooked and served by relatively inexpensive technicians rather than highly trained cooks. Although the Berni chain is long defunct, the underlying idea lives on in dining pubs. Indeed, dining pubs take the idea further as customers get their own drinks and order their own food, thereby cutting down on the need for waiting staff. Low-cost airlines have taken a similar approach by subtracting *frills* such as meals. *Pay as you go* mobile phone customers get a stripped-down version of the service afforded to contract customers.

Making things cheaper is called price competitiveness. Although ideally, quality and price competitiveness should be equally viable, price competitiveness tends to gain the upper hand, thanks to economies of scale. Cheaper things make making those cheap things even cheaper. It is a great cycle, as long as you are the one in it.

Key 7: Get the Price Right

Subtraction will make things cheaper, but it will not help you decide how much to charge. It is not just a matter of making something affordable; it has to fit the customer's budget. This is where psychology can help.

Budgeting is a way of compartmentalizing resources either mentally in our heads or on paper. We use budgets to help control expenditure: "so much for gas, so much for electricity" and so forth. Most of us carry around notional budgets in our heads. For example, we may decide that we will not pay more than, say, 20,000 dollars for a car, or 9.99 dollars for a paperback. Research by psychologists suggests that we are more likely to hesitate over buying something if it means breaking the budget.

Note that I did not say "if we cannot afford it." The customer may be a millionaire but still resistant to paying more than 9.99 dollars for a paperback book. In other words, if something is going to sell, the price must be within budget.

Economics also enters into the equation. Starbucks pays huge rents for their railway station kiosks, but that is not why their coffee is expensive.

The coffee is expensive because the kiosks are strategically positioned where you and I, in a hurry and eager for a caffeine *fix*, will pay inflated prices. The rents are high because landlords know the value of the location. The same principle explains why food and drink in convenience stores adjacent to railway stations are more expensive than less conveniently located stores. Commuters value their time and will therefore pay a premium for convenience. Moral: charge what the customer will bear.

That means being careful not to overcharge. After eating an expensive and indifferent burger from a high street chain, Wayne and his brother decided to *give it a go* by selling burgers, hot dogs, and fried chicken from a mobile van on an outdoor market. They decided to undercut chains by selling at 3.69 dollars instead of 4.60 dollars. It seemed foolproof, particularly as Wayne and his brother had gone to considerable trouble to create unique high-quality recipes, but no one bought. Wayne then reduced the price to match the typical market spend of 2.99 dollars. The result was astonishing, as Wayne recounts:

"We gave two pieces of chicken, chips and a drink like you get at _____."

Where they were $4.60, we were on at $3.59—but it just wasn't selling even though the product's fantastic, absolutely fantastic. We couldn't understand why it wouldn't go. So I says, 'It's the price.' Me [sic] brother says, 'But we're a pound cheaper than _____.'

I said, 'I know, but … three-dollar fifty odd is nearly four bucks.' So I said, 'Right! $2.99!' Me and brother said, 'it's too cheap, but we're still making decent money on it. So we put it on at $2.99 and within a week trade went mad.' '$2.99 for dinner! We'll have that!'

The same recently happened in big business. When ASUS launched the Eee PC with its 7-inch screen and Internet capability for 199 dollars, trade went mad. The product was originally designed for children, but by happy accident, it gave adults what they wanted too at a price well within budget.

Key 8: Add Value

Adding value is another possibility. The UK textile industry has largely succumbed to foreign competition, but there is still a market for specialty cloth. In fact, there is actually a shortage of weaving capacity in the United Kingdom.

You can buy a box of Faber–Castell pencils in a nice wooden box for around 70 dollars. A splendid way of adding value to a few bits of wood! Luxury stationers Smythson have done a similar thing for paper.

Entrepreneurially minded scientists are working on inventions to improve military combat dress. Armorers are creating bulletroof suits, for people want the security and the style. Existing suits of green and brown or sand-coloured desert do a reasonably good job of providing camouflage. They are detectable by the naked eye, however, particularly at close quarters. Scientists are currently experimenting with scientific discoveries into how human vision works to add value by making suits that are utterly invisible.

Another possibility is to repackage the mundane. There is nothing special about a bag of Granny Smith apples. Imagine, however, receiving rarer varieties packed in an attractive presentation box. You would probably be prepared to pay much more for the latter than the former, even though they are all apples. Adding value is the opposite side of the coin of reducing loss.

Customers will pay for mineral water in attractive bottles because it means they can place the bottle directly on to the table and avoid having to use a jug. This is why customers will pay more for two skinned chicken breasts than for a whole chicken. The point is, cutting and skinning adds value to the product out of all proportion to the cost of the labor involved.

Key 9: Invent a Name

What would you like for lunch? How about a piece of cheese, a piece of celery, a bit of bread, and a dab of chutney?

You wouldn't like it all? In that case, how about a ploughman's lunch?

When I run this exercise with MBA students, there are seldom any takers for the former, yet hands shoot up when I offer the latter! Which is odd, because they are the same thing.

We will probably never know the identity of the entrepreneurial genius who coined the term *ploughman's lunch*. The lesson is that there is money to be made in giving things an attractive name. In 1854, cholera erupted in the Soho area of London. A bright doctor named John Snow thought that the outbreak might be related to the water supply. He made a map of the area plotting the number of cases per household and marked the location of the wells. Dr Snow noticed that the highest density of cases centered upon a particular well, suggesting that this was the source of water contamination. Dr. Snow tested his hypothesis by removing the pump handle. The number of cases then fell drastically, suggesting that his theory was correct.

Over a century later, in May 1981, Peter Sutcliffe (known as the Yorkshire Ripper) was convicted of murdering 13 women and seriously injuring seven more between 1975 and 1980, though there may have been many other victims. Eventually, in late 1980, amid mounting concern over the police's continuing ineffectiveness, a special squad was formed to review the manhunt. A scientist attached to the team named Professor Stewart Kind was lying in his hotel bed unable to sleep for thinking about the case, when an idea suddenly struck him. Kind realized that the murderer would be under similar pressure to that faced by a wartime bomber, that is, to get home safely. Most of the attacks were committed in Leeds and Bradford with outliers in Huddersfield, Manchester, Halifax, and Keighley. Professor Kind reasoned that the further away from the murderer's home an attack happened, the earlier in the evening it was likely to be because of the greater distance to home, in order to minimize the risk of detection. He used this information to plot the center of gravity of the attacks rather as the 19th-century physician identified the suspect well. The results pointed to halfway between the Shipley and Manningham areas, a very close approximation, as it turned out.

Key 10: The Master Key

Ultimately, innovations stand or fall according to whether or not they gain (and retain) social acceptance. Some good ideas fail because people reject them. Screw caps on wine bottles are every bit as technically efficient as conventional corks and impart less loss to the customer, but only a few producers use them and then sometimes only on the slightly cheaper ranges. This is perhaps because consumers associate screw caps with poorer quality wines. Sometimes there seems to be no logical reason for acceptance or rejection. Video-style telephone facilities are nothing new. They first appeared in the early 1970s, but the idea was a commercial failure. For many years, even with improved technology, mobile telephone companies struggle to sell the service until the COVID-19 made almost impossible for people to get together. Suddenly, billions of people were using video-style telephone to interact with colleagues, friends, and family. Conversely, text messaging facilities were added to mobile phones as an afterthought, but they are actually more popular than voice calls. It seems bizarre when you consider the difficulties involved in *typing* out a text message. Only a tiny minority of mobile phones embody QWERTY keyboards, yet customers do not seem to mind the tortuous process. And look around on a bus or a train and you will see that the market for iPods extends far beyond teenagers.

If the time is not right, an idea may stall. When venture capitalists were seduced by the so-called dotcom boom, they rejected many better propositions. Politics too can enter the equation. Entrepreneurs who have tried to sell ideas such as cooling caps that prevent hair loss in patients being treated for cancer found themselves up against the medical establishment. Although the caps added only 10 dollars to the cost of treatment, doctors argued that they were too expensive. Conversely, there is little evidence that security cameras reduce crime, but now that we have them, there would probably be an outcry if they were removed. Gaining acceptance may involve dilution. The Spanish tourist resort Benidorm was once a fishing village. Falling air travel costs prompted the entrepreneurial mayor to develop (and ultimately overdevelop) the town as a holiday resort. The mayor succeeded, however, not by offering UK tourists authentic Spanish food and drink, but the familiar bacon and eggs plus the merest frisson of authenticity. Some Indian and Chinese restaurants (particularly in the early years) have also found dilution profitable.

It is possible to lose social acceptance as well as gain it, as evidenced, for example, by the downturn in the market for conventional light bulbs, battery-produced eggs, and plastic carrier bags. Events of September 11, 2001, seriously undermined global chains like McDonald's and Burger King, particularly in Third World countries, as the terrorist attacks destroyed social belief in things American. On the other hand, it was good news for local street sellers. Similarly, in 2020, Chinese companies and goods received the backlash due to the common belief that COVID-19 was originated in the Chinese government labs.

As to what gains acceptance that is anybody's guess! Gaining trust is important. Dell made home computers cheaper by selling through mail order, but it took years before customers learned to trust mail order. Indeed, Dell ended up paving the way for the rapid establishment of businesses such as Amazon and eBay.

Listening to customers can also help. This is where entrepreneurs have a head start over big business. Whereas executives sit in their offices all day studying statistics, entrepreneurs, particularly those at an early stage in their careers, are at the sharp end. They experience customer reactions first-hand. Ann, a young entrepreneur, planned to open a chain of shops. Lacking references and credentials, the only premises she could rent to open her first shop were in an economically deprived inner-city area. Ann invested a large portion of her precious capital in silver jewellery. Customer feedback soon told she had made a fundamental mistake.

Ann said, "Lower working class want to buy gold. They believe that if they're wearing gold, they look worth more. Even if it's the cheapest, nastiest gold they can get, they want gold!" So she gave them gold at $1.50 an item. It was indeed cheap and possibly nasty, but it was sold.

Chapter Summary

- Ask questions; the answers may be rewarding. There are great opportunities in plain sight, everyday annoyances, or small-scale issues that most people do not bother to look deeper into.
- Improving what already exists is a great way to innovate; you have a solid market, a solid reason for your consumers to buy your product, and an easy base to work off. Consumer convenience is a common way of improvising, from Blockbuster to Netflix, from button phones to touchscreens.
- Take what nobody wants; one man's trash is another's treasure. Aim to enter markets that barely have any significant competition, as those are the ones teeming with potential.
- Using good management, budgeting, and manufacturing techniques itself can be an innovation, from having more eco-friendly production processes, or lowering the cost of production or increasing the quality, or even just managing your finances better can lead to a potential business idea or a survivable startup.
- Specializing in niche or luxury industries or even advertising your business model is a viable way to go. Take a regular commodity and give the highest quality but pricey version of it.
- Naming is critical, as that is the face of your business. A name can lead to massive sales because people may be interested in the company or the product from its name.
- In the end, an idea survives if it gains market and social acceptance. If it doesn't, it has destined to fail. You can improve your product/idea acceptance by taking consumer feedback, market trials, and seeing market trends to realize where they tend, whether toward or away from products such as yours.

CHAPTER 3

Understanding and Figuring Out the Right Business Idea

The business idea is the foundation of a business. Ideas can be unique, and they can be ordinary. However present, they must be because without an idea, the business has no founding concept, no values, no consistency, and inevitably, no potential. An idea does not need to be great to do a successful business. It just needs to solve a problem or do something better.

> *In business, the idea is the main thing. Capital can be raised and lost and raised again, but lose the idea, and everything is lost.*
> —*Gottlieb Duttweiler*

> *Opportunity is missed by most because it is dressed in overalls and looks like hard work.*
> —*Thomas Edison*

Commercial business is not centered around sellers but instead centered around the buyers (consumers). This works by making sure the needs and wants of the consumers are matched with the passion and interests of the potential entrepreneur. Arriving at this stage can take much time, but the time will be worth it with proper diligence. The owner and operator of Equation Business Solutions in Cape Town, South Africa, says that exploring a subject or product that the entrepreneur is familiar with (or curious about) is an excellent place to begin. One can also explore other ideas by going through the yellow pages to find an existing idea that can be modified, expanded, or copied. Edwin Land, the inventor of Polaroid photography, once said that the best way to have a new idea is to stop thinking about old ideas. In this regard, perhaps combining different professions can yield a result. An interest in accounting and boating, for example, might be fused to provide accounting services to the boating industry. Alternatively, maybe experience with software and knowledge of transportation networks can be merged to create a new service for suppliers or distributors. Additional options include examining both sides of an existing opportunity. For instance, security and private police services make up the world's fastest-growing industry, so perhaps a copycat security service can be developed, or maybe a marketable idea that reduces the circumstances behind the need for more security is a better option.

Another way of searching for potential business ideas is to visit places with an economic level or geographic location of personal interest to find if people living there have one or two needs. It is also possible to investigate the business aspect of a field or subject with an exciting outlook.

The challenge for the entrepreneur is to match personal skills, interests, and capabilities with an inherent passion and tie it into an underserved customer base. Following is a list of questions designed to help do just that:

- **What do I enjoy doing the most?** Doing something enjoyable is an excellent way to ignite commitment and possibly uncover an idea that will prove profitable. For example, the Boeing (aircraft) company started after flight enthusiast Bill Boeing built a plane in 1916. One plane led to two, then three, and so on. In Glasgow, Scotland, child-lover Cathy Campbell turned the front room into a crèche (a daycare center). Cathy started small and insists she wants to stay small to focus on her clients and avoid too many administrative duties, thereby allowing her to do what she loves most, which is play with children.
- **What are my hobbies and interests?** Anything from growing roses to personalizing software programs to building model ships can be turned into a profitable business if the circumstances are right, either by teaching others how to do it, by packaging and selling what is created, or by selling related products to fellow enthusiasts. For example, several multi-million dollar computer companies (Apple, Dell, Microsoft, etc.) were started by *computer nerds* who turned

their computing interests into selling marketable computing products and services to similar enthusiasts.

- **What subject(s) or pastimes did I enjoy in college (or high school)?** Think back to your student years. Can the one or two subjects you found most fascinating be turned into a money-making idea? With a bit of thought and effort, they just might. For example, when MIT Professor Harold Edgerton invented the strobe light, he could not interest General Electric in its possibilities, so he hooked up with two students and formed a business (EG&G) that photographed mechanical processes at high speed, thereby providing a new way to look at, and solve industrial problems.

- Similarly, Hewlett-Packard was formed by two Stanford students (Dave Packard and Bill Hewlett) who had a passion for electronics. One of their first products, an audio oscillator, was purchased by Walt Disney to make Fantasia. Then there is Gary Comer—with no more than a high-school education and a love of sailing, Gary started a business that supplied sailing equipment to fellow enthusiasts. The name of that business—mail-order giant *Lands End*.

- **What marketable experience, knowledge, or skills do I possess?** Almost everyone possesses skill or knowledge that has the potential to make money. For example, Snap-On Tools began when machinists Joe Johnson and William Seidemann fashioned together interchangeable sockets and wrench handle to make their job easier. The company where they worked rejected their idea out of hand, but being experienced machinists, Johnson and Seidemann knew their idea was a sound one, so they developed it independently. In another example, fast-food manager R. David Thomas helped Colonel Sanders succeed with his Kentucky Fried Chicken franchise, then went on to use the additional experience he gained to start Wendy's burger chain (named after his daughter). Further examples of using personal skills to create a new business include mash-up operations that combine different Web-based tools to create new search and software

possibilities or teaching-based operations that show others
how to use digital photo software (or any new software for
that matter). Technical processing of data collection services
and services that provide creative design work for documents,
menus, or marketing provide additional examples.

- **Have I ever looked at another business or product and
thought, "I can do better than that!?"** Many successful
businesses get started because they are better than their
competitors offer in terms of service, quality, location, speed, or
uniqueness. When Kemmons Wilson was charged an additional
fee at a roadside motel for each of his five children, he became
so upset that he started Holiday Inn. Polish immigrant Rueben
Mattus, a high-school dropout who scratched a meager living
selling ice cream in Brooklyn, New York, suffered through years
of price wars, cut-throat competition, and ingredient shortages
caused by World War II before he finally decided to fight his
competitors by developing an ice cream that did not skimp
on ingredients. After concluding that many people in America
hated the Irish, the Italians, the Poles, and the Jews, Mattus
came up with the fictitious Danish-sounding name of Haagen-
Dazs (he reasoned that no one hated the Danes) and took
over a niche luxury-food market that had previously not been
considered. In New York, dry-cleaning equipment salesman
Leon Hirsch was milling around a patent broker's office when
he noticed an ungainly surgical stapler that had been invented
decades earlier. Fascinated, he bought the licensing rights to the
tool, improved its performance, and started The United States
Surgical Corporation (it became a Fortune 500 company).
Simply put, people will usually pay good money for products
or services that, in some way, improve upon what is currently
on the market.

- **Are the people in my community asking for or in need of
a product or service?** For centuries, perceptive entrepreneurs
have known that products or services needed or wanted are
sure-fire moneymakers. That is how Levi Strauss (of *blue
jeans* fame) got his start in the clothing industry. Strauss

immigrated to the United States to start a dry goods business, but after landing in California, he quickly discovered that most miners were desperate for clothing that could withstand the rigors of the mining trade. Not wanting to pass up this opportunity (and not finding anything on the market to fit the bill), he fashioned a pair of trousers out of the canvas, used rivets to hold the seams together, and created the *501 Blue Jean*. Avon Cosmetics was founded by book salesman David McConnell who quickly discovered that the free perfume samples he gave to women were more popular than his books. Decades later, Tom Fatjo and Louis Walters sensed that changing environmental laws were going to create opportunities for garbage collection, so they bought a specialized garbage truck to help fill the needs of their community. Thirteen years passed, during which time their business, Browning–Ferris, became the second-largest waste disposal company in America. Lastly, the Kaiser supermarket in Berlin, Germany, realized that most of the city's population would be over the age of 50 by 2010, is now raking in newfound profits, thanks to a store designed specifically for the elderly. The store includes non-slip floors, wider aisles, magnifying glasses attached to shopping carts (to help read product labels), and steps lining the aisles so that customers can reach items on high shelves.

- **What is that thing that will make the world (or my neighborhood) a better place?** New ways of thinking that can help the world become a better place to live can lead to much entrepreneurial success. For example, Anita Roddick founded the Body Shop because she was upset that most cosmetics were tested on animals by squirting chemicals directly into their eyes. Her idea was to set up a company that sold beauty products free from animal testing. One hundred years earlier, the Borden food company came up with a winning idea that made the world safer when founder Gail Borden witnessed several infant deaths from putrefied milk and saw the need for a non-perishable substitute.

Borden's creative thinking and determination led to the discovery of condensed milk. The clockwork radio, a wind-up device invented by Trevor Baylis, so people in remote places (without access to batteries) can stay in touch with the rest of the world, became a worldwide testament to innovation and persistence (a wind-up laptop computer has also been developed based on this concept). The water-purifying drinking straw, packed with filtration aids, is yet another life-saving device designed to assist people in times of need. Over the past few decades, farmers and livestock breeders have capitalized on markets that pay top prices for eco-friendly, organic products. The point here is that opportunities exist for entrepreneurs who invent or innovate new products or services, increase efficiency, develop safe product alternatives, improve work systems or manufacturing processes, or find ways to produce products that are easier on the environment and healthier for customers.

- **Is there an obvious problem out there just waiting for a solution?** With so many people concerned about clean, cheap energy (and the environment), business ventures that provide an alternative to dirty and expensive energy practices are proving to be real money-spinners. For example, in 2005, Scottish entrepreneur David Gordon was exiting a meeting in Glasgow, Scotland, when he noticed a tree swaying in the wind next to an apartment building. He began thinking about how the energy moving the tree could be harnessed to provide power for the building, and he quickly realized that somebody somewhere would probably make a fortune from wind power. He wanted that someone to be him. After doing some research, Gordon visualized a wind turbine small enough to fit on the top of a house or building. His next move was to develop a patented *inverter* that pumps the turbine's electricity straight into a building's power structure. A range of products and services followed to complement the sustainable energy sector capitalizing on—including offering customers help with financing. The result—in his first year of business, Gordon sold over 18,000 Windsave turbines at a price of around 4,400 dollars per unit, but it has not been smooth sailing; the company experienced many ups and downs along its way due to the pioneering aspect of its product. Indeed, due to a series of quality control issues and other problems, it is difficult to ascertain if the company is still in business.

- Meanwhile, in Eskilstuna, Sweden, a new shopping mall (ReTuna Återbruksgalleria) opened in early 2017. The facilities contain both a recycling center and a shopping mall. Customers can donate the items that they no longer need and shop for something new all in one stop. Dropped-off goods are sorted into various workshops where they are refurbished or repaired accordingly. Products are sorted into 14 specialty shops: furniture, computers, audio equipment, clothes, toys, bikes, gardening, and building materials, all garnered from second-hand products. The center also includes a café and restaurant focusing on organic products and a conference and exhibition facility complete with a school for studying recycling.

- **Is there any current product or service available in the market that has my trust?** The fundamental truth is that not all business ideas have to be original. Sometimes a pre-existing idea can be copied, modified, and restructured to form a new market. Doing this can have a great return that will be astonishing. For example, after witnessing Domino's Pizza's quick home deliveries in his travels through the United States, Leopoldo Pujals returned to Spain, set up a similar operation in 1987, and named it TelePizza. By 2010, the company had opened 1,025 outlets around the world. In April 2016, the company completed an IPO worth around 550 million euros. In the United States, Cheri Faith Woodward started the Faith Mountain Company, a 20-million-dollar mail-order business that distributes herbs, dried flowers, kitchen implements, and handicrafts. Although Woodward learned her trade from a local woman sharing her knowledge with others for decades, Woodward turned this knowledge into a business. After 25 years of business, the company closed and sold its mailing list and database, which contained the names and addresses of over 1.7 million customers.

- **What do the people or customers in my current job complain about (or want) the most?** Unhappy customers can unwittingly uncover vast opportunities—if they are taken seriously and if someone takes the time to listen to them. For example, Buster Brown shoes came into being when shoe salesman George Warren Brown heard people complaining that most shoe fashions were staid. At this point (1878), the entire American shoe industry was located in New England, so Brown developed a line of shoes that catered to his local market. Within a few years, his products were being sold coast to coast. More recently, a corporate executive in London, England, overheard several complaints circulating in his office about how difficult it was to find a good plumber. Intrigued by the notion of setting out on his own and working with his hands, he took a course in plumbing, became a registered plumber, and set up his own business. He then makes about the same money per year as a plumber compared to what he made as an executive.

- **Is there a need for a product or service in an underserved market?** Business communities ignore too many small markets because of prejudice, ignorance, outdated misconceptions, or just plain laziness. Consider the GrameenPhone telecommunications company in Bangladesh, which was assisted in its start-up phase by Nobel Prize winner Mohammad Yunus. GrameenPhone (*gram* means village) began selling mobile phones to impoverished communities in 1997. Instead of sticking with the traditional business model of selling one phone at a time to a customer (which is impossible to do in a country where the average yearly income is only 286 dollars), a new business model was established in which a single mobile phone is leased to a village and shared by dozens of people. Six years later, with this innovative service has expanded to include over 50 million people, GrameenPhone produced revenues of 330 million dollars per annum. Future revenues are expected to rise to half a billion dollars. Equally important, by providing poor regions with much-needed phone service, farmers and local business people can now sell their products on a timelier basis. The resulting rise in income levels has lifted many customers out of abject squalor—and all because an astute entrepreneur named Iqbal Qadir took the time to figure out how the selling of a helpful product could be modified to fit a needy market.

- **Is there a type of person, group, or customer base I connect with?** Those who enjoy working with the elderly, an ethnic group, hobbyists, children, mountain climbers, basketball players, or any form of potential customer probably harbor an above-average ability to talk with them, discover what they need, or want, and learn ways to serve them. That is how Daniel Gerber, son of the President of the Fremont Canning Company in Michigan, came up with his revolutionary idea of selling baby food. Gerber never thought much about parents with small children until his wife had a baby. Only then did he realize how difficult it was to prepare and strain baby food. After confirming this with countless parents, he used his father's machinery to develop food products for infants. Eventually, his idea became so successful that the company abandoned its adult line and concentrated solely on making baby food. In another example, the all-female Pink Taxi service in Moscow, Russia, began when entrepreneur Olga Fomina discovered that many women do not like to ride in taxis because most taxi drivers are men, and men are the perpetrators of most assaults on women. Her business idea was to start a taxi service that only caters to women—a business model that has spawned similar all-female taxi businesses in many other countries.

How Dumb Is a Dumb Idea?

As said earlier, fear is a significant hindrance that can frustrate all entre-preneurial goals or processes. Also, unfounded beliefs or the opinions of others should not serve as a barrier to starting a business before proper research is carried out.

The moment a business idea has been birthed, profound research is the best thing to do, as this would allow the potential entrepreneur to know if the idea can be sustained or viable. This was stated by the operator of South Africa's Cape Town Boat Builder's Initiative. This means that the potential market for the business is profoundly examined to know if the demand for the product or service is excellent enough to cater to the cost of production while also sustaining long-term profitability. A thorough research investigation will provide valuable information as to how a product can be modified to maximize profits, how it can best be sold, the price customers are willing to pay for it, the size of the market, or, perhaps, the painful truth that the idea is simply not feasible. One of the best examples of this point is the dog poop collection industry (yes, that was correct).

Collecting dog excrement may seem strange to make a living, yet over 300 such businesses exist in North America alone. With 8–10 dollars being charged to clean up a typical household yard, and the number of dog owners increasing, profits are—excuse the pun—piling up. In fact, by June 2010, one company (Pet Butler) in Texas serviced 50,000 clients and collected more than 500,000 dollars every week (as of May 2017, the company boasts that it has *scooped* over 24,254,962 poops!).

At the very far end of the spectrum, rethink and consider the success of the Starbuck coffee shops. When you think and go back to the 1970s when Starbucks was launched, it seemed unreasonable to create a business model based on a coffee shop where the price of a coffee cup was placed at five or six dollars. This model was created when many shops were mainly selling theirs for a higher amount. Millions of potential customers, however, thought otherwise. The moral of the story? Do not *pooh-pooh* a business idea that targets a bona fide customer base and satisfies a need.

The Need to Create New Ideas Will Always Persist— Advice From Experienced Entrepreneurs

Even after running a successful business for years, at some point, whatever is being sold—as well as the way it is being sold—may become tiresome in the eyes of customers. Therefore, it makes sense to be on the lookout for new products to sell and new ways to add to or improve existing products and services. The good news is that entrepreneurs do not have to go through this process alone. Good, reliable ideas can (and should) come from many different sources if an effort is made to find them.

- When a business idea is conceived, ignore the pessimists, and rely on research. Entrepreneurs often succeed by breaking the rules, which means going against the conventional wisdom of people who have no proof to back up their opinions.
- Even if your business has been up and running for years, never stop thinking about refining old ideas and coming up with new ones.
- It is better to have a million ideas and no money than a million dollars and no ideas. A pile of money with no ideas to nurture it will soon be lost.
- Dare to be different. Those who travel with the herd often end up where the herd is going, usually nowhere.
- Be prepared to compromise. This is not a contradiction to the preceding statements. Commercial business is about serving customers, not the whims and self-interest of a business owner.
- Allow research rather than opinion to determine the difference between a good idea, a fantasy, a scam, or a terrible idea.

There is never the right idea until proven correct by a lot of homework and research. Read and find out what could work for your idea. Also, be sure to weigh the pros against the cons before investing time and money in a new idea. If you search deeply and thoroughly, you will find that no idea is new. Therefore, make use of the information you get and use it to your advantage. Remember, the customers are the first set of people to think about for any business.

Chapter Summary

- Businesses are centered around the consumer. If consumers do not like your product, there is no business. You reach a stage where you have a purchasing audience, and a steady income is a journey of its own.
- There are personal questions you need to ask as an entrepreneur, "Is this the right industry for me to get into?" or "Am I capable of doing this?" or "Do I enjoy this type of work?," and such questions are essential to ask before you make any sort of actual actions into entering into an industry or implementing an idea. They will help you filter out what is best for you and help you make the most informed and rational decision possible.
- No idea is too dumb if it has market viability. People have made fortunes from the littlest of things. If there is money to be made and a good fit for you, go for it.

CHAPTER 4

Deciding to "Give it a Go"— How NOT to Do It?

Starting a new business is very common, and therefore, new businesses fail often and miserably. Out of all of the reasons, the most common one is timing. Why? Because selling a product when the market is not ready is a death wish, the only problem is that most start-ups do not know when they are "ready." Adequate market research, patience, and good decision making can overcome this, but this is not the only reason, there are many more, as discussed and resolved in the chapter.

Starting a business is like deciding to have a baby; it requires great mental strength and preparedness; venturing into the process with fears and not knowing what to expect can crumble everything within a twinkle of an eye. There is not a man without fears; the only difference between those living scared and those living above their fears are based on their will to proceed and their will to face their fears.

Before deciding to go on with your startup, it is essential to know the fears attached to being a successful startup. The four significant fears of entrepreneurship are discussed as follows.

The Four Main Fears of Entrepreneurship

The number of qualities and attributes needed to succeed in business is quite extensive. So, does that mean an entrepreneur needs to be a super-hero to triumph in the business world?

Not. Few people are born with all the marvelous abilities that are needed to succeed in life. Nevertheless, successful business owners appear to get around their shortcomings by learning as they go, admitting their frailties, and shoring up their weaknesses—a process that helps overcome their fears. Fear is a common emotion that often manifests itself into excuses, procrastination, or inaction. Indeed, many psychologists say that fear is the root cause of most human problems. Listed next are four of the most common fears associated with starting a business:

(a) **Age:** Exactly what age is too old or too young to run a business? Years ago, the owner of a sporting goods store in the United States celebrated his 100th birthday (he opened his enterprise in 1933). He was only working four hours a day, but he was still working and introducing new products and beating his competitors. Colonel Sanders, the man who invented Kentucky Fried Chicken, began selling his secret formula to franchisees at 64. Ray Kroc, a malt-shake machine salesman from Illinois, bought four California hamburger restaurants when he was 52 years old and re-tooled them into the McDonald's. Thus, it goes as the number of entrepreneurs over the age of 50 is expected to rise dramatically, according to industry experts.

At the other end of the scale, Michael Dell, the founder of Dell Computer, began his first business at 13. By the time he turned 19, the computer parts business he had run out of his college dorm room had grossed 80,000 dollars per month. Not to be outdone, Bill Gates started Microsoft at the tender age of 19. Furthermore, today, millennials are starting businesses at almost twice the rate of their older peers. The overall message is that age is not a determinant factor in starting and running a business. Attitude, courage, and action are far more critical.

(b) **Lack of money:** There is no single lie that start-up businesses will flourish without so much of a hassle if there is enough money. Money makes things happen faster, but you need more than money to make your startup a success. Some entrepreneurs who have had the experience even claim that it is best to start up a business with small capital as possible. The belief attached to this is that when some new business owners start with plenty of cash, they tend to waste it on things they do not need. For example, they rent an office, get expensive computers, employ a secretary who is not readily needed for a start, and many more.

(c) Additionally, having a small amount of money to start a business will teach tenacity, efficiency, and frugality. This idea may not convince you, but with the following examples, you should be convinced. This set of people started their business with little chumps of money, and because they had the desire to succeed, they did all they could to make it work. For example, Disney, Apple, Hewlett Packard, and the Mattel toy company all began life in garages. Seattle-based teenager Jim Casey founded UPS with 100 dollars, two bicycles, one telephone, and six employees. The Nike Corporation began in 1964 when Phil Knight and Bill Bowerman each invested 300 dollars in a shipment of athletic shoes and sold them out of a car at track meets. Eighteen-year-old Joyce C. Hall started the Hallmark greeting card company with an armful of postcards he kept in two shoeboxes. Thomas Monaghan, who spent his early life in and out of orphanages and foster homes (and was kicked out of everything afterward from a Catholic seminary to the Marine Corps) started Dominos Pizza by turning a bankrupt pizza parlor—half of which he traded for his Volkswagen Beetle—into the United States's number one pizza delivery service. Moreover, the Marriott Hotel chain began its life as a humble root beer stands in 1927.

Simply put (as the old saying goes), business success is usually based on 10 percent capital and 90 percent guts. Stated another way, people who cannot make money without money usually will not make money. According to successful business practitioners, mind power, diligence, and passion are far more influential.

(d) **Fear of rejection:** A significant number of the most successful business owners today have all readily admitted that the road to prosperity comes with much rejection. Indeed, many thick-boned entrepreneurs have openly stated that they failed not once, twice, but several times before they made headway. This brings the question of how they end up becoming successful with their business? The answer to this is they have found a way to deal with their failures and adversity by choosing not to brood. Instead, they chose to move on and make good fortune for themselves in the long run. For example, Bernard Marcus and Arthur Blank, who, in 1978, joined forces with co-worker Ronald Brill and founded Home Depot—after all three men had lost their jobs in a corporate buyout. Alternatively, consider King C. Gillette, the inventor of the safety razor, who suffered six years of humiliating rejection from companies, investors, and toolmakers while they laughed out loud at his innovative new product. When King eventually decided to produce his invention himself, sales rose at a rate of 1,000 percent annually! The story of Ewing Kauffman provides another excellent example of how successful entrepreneurs rebound from rejection. Shortly after the World War II, Kauffman was fired from his job as a salesman because his commissions exceeded the President's salary at the company where he worked. Undaunted, he descended into his basement and began making calcium pills from oyster shells. Years later, after capturing 40 percent of the 100-million-dollar calcium supplement market, he sold his company to Dow Chemical for a fortune.

Such bounce-back stories are not the stuff of old-fashioned motivational stories. Indeed, millennials seem more prone than their elders to learn from failure, brush it off, and then parlay it into victory. The lesson here is that winning often lies in the mind. Success to those with the perseverance to stay in the game is usually nothing more than failure turned inside out.

(e) **Lack of education and experience:** There is evidence that suggests a college education does not guarantee business success. Indeed, it sometimes appears otherwise. Steven Jobs and Stephen Wozniak, for example, founded Apple Computer after dropping out of college. Neither one of them had any entrepreneurial experience. Michael Dell, the multimillionaire founder of Dell Computer, is also a college dropout. The same goes for Ted Waitt, who, after quitting school, underwent nine months of on-the-job training at a computer company only to leave and start Gateway 2000. Ten years later, his salary exceeded 500,000 dollars per annum. John Bond, former chairman of HSBC (one of the world's largest banks), also never went to university.

Still not convinced? Then consider the story of Ian Leopold, whose college Professor failed him because of the unrealistic business plan he submitted in class. Leopold turned a 48-dollar investment into four million dollars in 10 years with the same plan (writing university guidebooks).

In the last years of her life, multimillionaire Anita Roddick, founder of The Body Shop, advised entrepreneurs to "stay away from business schools." She believed that business schools focus too much on the financial side of the business and ignore the all-important human element.

Of course, this does not mean that education and experience are not needed to start and run a business. The following statement was relayed to me several years ago by a successful entrepreneur in France: "I did not learn any ground-breaking secrets in business school," he said. "Most of what I have learned I experienced on the job. However, one thing I have noticed over the years is that no matter where business studies are taught, the folks who need this information the most are usually nowhere to be found." His point is that there is no shame in not knowing everything there is about running a business. There is only shame in not admitting it and ignoring the need to improve.

> The afore-listed fears are not there to make you stay back, but to know when to start because there is never a good time to start. Follow the following outlines to make your way to the top very straightforward.

It Is Sometimes Good to Learn the Hard Way!

A good idea for business is important, but it is not enough. Just as in academia, there are interesting questions and there are researchable questions, in business, there are good ideas and ideas that are good and commercially viable.

The statistics on new business startups are frightening. Fewer than 20 percent survive beyond two years. Moreover, when new businesses collapse, the results are often financially and emotionally devastating.

Nor are experienced entrepreneurs immune from failure. Almost all tell stories about deals that soured, about contracts that lost money and opportunities that became liabilities sometimes with disastrous consequences.

Yet, many failures are avoidable.

Obviously, you will never know for certain whether an idea is viable until you try. It is axiomatic that all decisions involving uncertainty run the risk of failing. No matter how carefully you plan and research a prospective venture, there are no cast-iron guarantees of success. The trouble is, what defeats many fledgling and experienced entrepreneurs is not the hazards of *war* so much as the certainties of common sense.

To be more precise, failure often reflects errors of judgment. Such errors are what psychologists call systematic. That is, we believe we know what causes them, how they are likely to bias decision making, and how to correct them.

The Illusion of Control

The Master allows things to happen. She shapes events as they come. She steps out of the way and lets the Tao speak for itself.

—*Laozi*

Imagine choosing a lottery card. Which option would you prefer (assume the shopkeeper is honest), to accept a card from the shopkeeper or to choose the card yourself? Logically it makes no difference which option you choose. The statistical probabilities of winning are identical. Yet, you may have elected to choose the card yourself because intuitively you feel you are more likely to win if you do. The term was coined by the psychologist Ellen Langer, the illusion of control refers to our tendency to overestimate our ability to influence outcomes, even in those outcomes where we have none.

Humans create this illusion as something to back or give grounding to your choices. It is always your choice to choose the card yourself or let the shopkeeper do it, but the fact that you are choosing it creates a false sense of security, as if choosing the card yourself will lead to a more favorable outcome. The illusion simply solves the problem of whom to blame if you lose, and that person is yourself.

In 1982, distinguished psychologist Shelley Taylor published a fascinating book named *Positive Illusions*, which suggested, among other things, that depression might not actually be seeing things as worse than they are, but, rather, seeing them as they are. Taylor's thesis is that we are out of touch with reality to begin with! According to Taylor, most people have an overly inflated idea of their own competence, as evidenced, for example, by our slavish adherence to the daily *to-do* list. Almost every time we compile such a list, we seriously overestimate what we can accomplish in a single day. Moreover, we never learn. Having accomplished only a fraction of the tasks that we set ourselves, undaunted we go and make another list!

This happens due to a disconnect between your actual performance and your expected performance. Just like a tired athlete who may set the bar lower for one day to accomplish their goals still, we raise our expectations but lower the bar, creating a gap between what is being done and how much should be finished. This gap can also be due to the illusion of control, where we think and blindly assume that we are doing equal to the amount we expect and the amount that happens. We think that we control what we do ourselves and how much, but in reality, we are pretty much in the dark when tracking progress.

Up to a point, illusions of control are a good thing. If you thought too deeply and seriously about all the risks involved in starting and running a business, you might never try. Indeed, it is often the realists who quit first when the going gets rough precisely because they can see only too well that the odds are against them. Paradoxically, optimists may win through in the end because they have no idea of what they are up against!

But only up to a point. Ultimately, there are concrete realities to be addressed. Hitler made this mistake when he invaded Russia. He insisted that the troops could fight effectively in sub-zero temperatures without proper winter clothing. No matter how much Hitler berated his generals, it made no difference. His tanks could not move without petrol. His soldiers could not march without sufficient food. Likewise, entrepreneurs need a cash flow: they need to sell enough to meet expenses, restock, and perhaps repay loans. Where is the money going to come from?

An illusion of control creates, as said before, a false sense of security. You assume that everything is fine, the money will come in, and everything is under control. Nevertheless, the reality can be very different. Realism is one of the most valuable tools of a good investor and a great entrepreneur. Although optimism will create motivation, it will not run your business. Every cost must be seen with cynicism. You should always know if you are winning or losing; telling yourself that you are winning when you are knee-deep in overdue bills is a death sentence.

The Overconfidence Trap

These are vital questions. Yet, overconfident entrepreneurs may not stop to ask them. Why else do people buy pubs that have already had a succession of owners who have gone bankrupt? They do it because they believe they can make a difference, though usually they just end up bankrupt too.

Overconfidence can manifest itself in other ways. Michael bought a business that he had worked in for five years. He knew (or should have known) that it was taking very little money; that was why the owner was selling it so cheaply. Instead of confronting the problem and thinking about whether and, if so, how he could achieve a turnaround, Michael simply put up a notice saying "Under New Management," as if that alone would suffice. He lasted just 16 weeks.

Being overconfident is how you jump into the red. As said before and again and again, optimism and being a visionary are excellent and necessary, but they will not run a business. It would help if you thoroughly scrutinized a business plan before you even think about implementing it.

For example, Jessica invests in a small insurance firm. For her, insurance looks like an accessible business; she is *optimistic*; it is banking, but withdrawals are incredibly infrequent, proper? The demand for it is high, and the costs "are not that bad." She invests 50,000 dollars into it, and she loses all of it in a year. Why? Insurance fraud. Surprisingly, Jessica did not realize that fraud in the insurance industry was widely prevalent, and that investigating faulty claims costs a lot. She had decided to focus more on consumer service and a website, so most of her money went to that. When faulty claims started coming in, she drowned in losses and had to shut the business down.

Dreaming With Discipline

When I recount these stories to my MBA students, someone usually asks, "Didn't they have a business plan?" In my experience, entrepreneurs who fail typically make one of three mistakes, namely:

1. They have no plan at all.
2. Their plan is not properly thought through.
3. They *fiddle* the figures until the plan makes financial sense.

The mechanics of business plans are beyond the scope of this book. What I can say, however, is that, done properly, a plan is a good way of testing reality, thereby helping to avoid the overconfidence trap because the process of planning forces you to consider whether your ideas are practical. The trouble is that the most important element of the plan is ultimately guesswork. You can usually estimate costs with reasonable accuracy. More difficult is estimating how many customers there will be and how long it will take for the business to become established. Starting a new venture, *giving it a go*, whether it is a completely new foray into business or branching out from an existing business, can be very exciting. When we feel strongly committed to something, we can develop blind spots, paying more attention to information that supports our preconceived notion while downplaying or even ignoring contradictory information. Some entrepreneurs go into business with no plan, no idea what to expect, and therefore nothing to measure success or failure against. Others embark upon business with half a plan, as we shall see later in this chapter, with key elements such as cash flow projections missing. Another problem is what we call *gaming*; increasing prices or bumping up the anticipated level of custom until it all makes sense on paper, that is. It is only when the business starts to travel the rocky road of reality that those optimistic projects start to unravel. Incidentally, once you become established in business, you may well receive requests from would-be and other established entrepreneurs for financial support. Some of these opportunities will be worth pursuing. The majority are likely to be *no-brainers*. It was one of the Rothschilds, I think, who said that if he had pursued even a fraction of the opportunities that were offered to him, he would have been rapidly ruined. Treat such investment opportunities with healthy skepticism. Ask the same questions that a bank manager or venture capitalist would ask of you, such as:

- How much is the prospective owner proposing to invest in the idea?
- Who else is involved?
- At face value, does the idea seem credible?
- What market research has been conducted and with what results?

- How comprehensive and well thought-out is the business plan?
- Does the prospective owner have the requisite skills and experience to run the business?
- Does the prospective owner have the requisite energy and commitment to go the distance?

The Dangers of Myopia

Insufficient reality testing may result in myopia that prevents us from seeing a complete and accurate picture. For example, Sam explains the rationale for his first business—"a franchised outlet selling trinkets costing $1; I think people will pay if cheap. There are other [similar] businesses [that] charge $5. $5 is too much for some people to pay—so I think that if I just charge $1 people will buy." First Saturday, he made 900 dollars. At first blush, Sam's strategy appears sound: he is competing on price, with a clear rationale of appealing to the less affluent shoppers. Further probing reveals a fundamental flaw, however, as Sam has really only got half of a business plan. Sam again: "Now is Tuesday and people only look, they don't buy. Already they ask, 'When is new stock coming in?' Given that the new stock only came in the previous day (Monday), the downturn seems ominous. The novelty value of the business has already passed and people are visiting not to buy but merely for entertainment. How will Sam fare the next Saturday, and the Saturday after that? Myopia resides in failing to consider the other side of the equation. People may buy, but what about the rent of 500 dollars a week plus business rates and all the other expenses? Sam needs to make 900 dollars every Saturday just to cover expenses and replenish stock. Then, he has an assistant to pay. Assuming he breaks even, he and his business partner receive nothing. Is that sustainable and, if so, for how long?

"In business there are risks. But there are also certainties."

The point is, none of this is hidden from Sam. No uncertainty surrounds the rent and other expenses. He has placed too much reliance upon his pricing strategy and not thought enough about the practicalities of implementing it.

Recall: A good idea for business is not enough. When Marcia was made redundant, she decided to turn a problem into an opportunity to exploit her specialist knowledge by opening a takeaway business selling exotic cuisine. In principle, it was a promising scheme because it would be difficult for competitors to imitate. But Marcia too had only half a plan as she neglected cash flow and in particular the cost of supplies until the business was under way. Marcia said: I was like, "Oh my God! I didn't realize it would be so expensive." "Just the meat alone because we do special mutton: now mutton is not something that is easy to get hold of, and when you do get it, it's expensive. And we were buying that every single day even though you're selling [sic] … it's every day you have to replace it, it's quite a lot of money." Again there was no uncertainty about the price of mutton. Marcia ended up learning the hard way because she failed to think through in sufficient detail how the business would operate in practice. There is no substitute for mapping out an idea in detail. If you cannot afford to buy stock, the blunt reality is that you have no business.

It is also very important to research the local market. What is the going rate for goods and services? Another mistake made by Marcia was that in order for her to create a seemingly viable business plan, her prices were significantly above the average customer mental/financial budget. She then discovered that not enough people were buying her albeit delicious food, so she raised the price in order to meet her expenses but, in fact, only compounded her difficulties.

Denial

As human beings, we are adept at hearing good news and equally adept at shutting out bad news. As denial occurs unconsciously, we may believe that we have done our homework, asked all the right questions, and weighed the answers. In fact, it may be that nothing is further from the truth.

"Better to begin with doubts and end in certainties than begin with certainties and end in doubts."

Carole ran a profitable business selling reconditioned televisions and videos. As new sets became cheaper, she realized that she needed to look elsewhere for the mainstay of her business. She decided to diversify into the *one-hour* dry-cleaning business. It was an enormous investment, but Carole was confident that it would succeed because there was a constant stream of passing trade and no competition nearby. Carole said, "The people who sold it did not promise that it was going to make a fortune. They said that it was a good thing to augment a business that was already established. Everything that they said was true in actual fact. But I believed that being where the footfall was so great, we couldn't fail. I felt that we were really on to a winner."

Notice what happens here. The company marketing the equipment behave ethically as they explain the limitations of the business. Carole, however, glossed over the point. The result is an enormous gap between expectations and reality concerning a critically important investment decision: "I thought that [dry cleaning] would be a good money-spinner. In actual fact it wasn't—it was poor. It's very labour-intensive for little return… That was a huge gamble, which did not pay off." In fact, the business generated just enough money to cover the repayments on the loan. Carole said, "We forgot the main thing about people. They'll see what they expect to see. And we were invisible. They didn't see because they didn't expect to see. You will get people coming to you, after four years people that you see day in, day out would bring me a suit to clean and they would say, 'Never noticed you here, didn't realize that you did dry cleaning.' I paid $100,000 for the equipment and I got $1,500 for it when I sold it. So that was a major blow to my finances."

It is a speculative point, but we may be most susceptible to making erroneous decisions like Carole's when things are not going well and an apparent solution to our problems suddenly appears. Again, speculatively, we may also be propelled into bad decisions when we have been searching unsuccessfully for a solution for a long time and end up pouncing upon something (anything) just to end the pain of indecision.

Too Good to Lose?

Some successful entrepreneurs claim to rely solely upon intuition when making important decisions. In other words, they dispense with analysis and certainly never bother with writing business plans. We will see in the next chapter that intuition does have an important role to play in decision making. The danger I wish to highlight here, however, is that what we call intuition may be merely wishful thinking. If, like Carole, you believe that an idea can hardly fail, treat that belief as a danger signal. Luck does play a part in business, but be aware that susceptibility to myopia is also heightened when an opportunity seems to be too good to miss. This is because we are liable to be dazzled by all the advantages of the idea and therefore neglect to probe the potential hazards. Sue was offered a large consignment of cheap t-shirts. On paper, it looked an admirable proposition. Buy for 0.25 dollars and sell for 2.99 dollars. Before reading on, pause awhile and evaluate this proposition. Is it a good idea? What snags can you think of? "I won't ever go down that road again," said Sue. "Why?" I asked. "Didn't they sell?" Sue replied, "Oh yeah, we sold 'em. We sold 'em all day long. I had this stack on t'floor."

"You think how much you've got to sell at $2.99 to make $400 and how much work there is. A major mistake; we did sell 'em, yeah, but with the effort that went into selling at $2.99, I could have gone out and sold a bloody Ferrari quicker. Then everybody wanted everything for $2.99. So, it killed everything else. [People] came up, 'Is that $2.99, is that $2.99?' And we're still getting it now. I won't ever go down that road again."

Faced with a seemingly windfall opportunity, Sue seized it without thinking about how the decision might play out in practice. She probably could not have foreseen that this *Del Boy* opportunity would *kill everything else*, but a grain of imagination would have shown the floor piled up with crates of t-shirts, and a calculation on the back of an envelope would have revealed how much work would be involved in making 400 dollars and given Sue pause to question whether this was such a good idea after all.

Another excellent example of this is Blockbuster. They quoted themselves that they were "too big to lose." They were unable to catch up to consumer demand and ultimately had to shut down.

Chapter Summary

- The four fears of entrepreneurship are age, a lack of financial wealth, a fear of rejection, and a lack of education and experience.
- These fears are significant deterring factors, but they should not be because the concerns raised by these fears are not valid. You are never too old to start a business, nor are you ever too poor. If your idea is good enough, investors, banks, and customers will come. Rejection is a staple of life, and even more common in the business world, it is something everyone will or has faced. A lack of education and experience can be fixed by studying markets and researching; you do not need to be a PhD in economics to see if x sells more than y and understand why it does.
- Be mindful of the illusion of control, you may seem like you are performing as you expected, but the reality can be very different. Trust the numbers over yourself.
- As the common saying goes, "too much of anything can bring harm," too much confidence can bring harm by letting you make irrational decisions and take unnecessary and uncalculated risks.
- A rock-solid business plan is the heart of your startup; it allows you to dream with discipline. Sketch out your ideas, new production methods or products, how you will manage things, and then back it up with numbers. If you cannot, ditch the idea. The market is not kind to the fools who put in their money believing in a false reality.
- Limited research and market testing, limited understanding of the industry and the product can lead you to sail blind, blind into an endless ditch.
- Do not gloss over details when looking at potential investments and ideas; the devil is in the details.
- Nothing is ever too big to fail; horrible ideas are like black holes of cash and time; they will drain you away from promising ventures and give nothing in return.

CHAPTER 5

Optimal Solutions—How to Choose Between Alternatives

Good decisions are what keep a business running. These make the entrepreneur essential and valued because, without good decision making, a trillion-dollar idea can fall into ruin within minutes. There must be a balance, as in all things, of risk and reward. Depending on the type of business and the interests of its owners, this can vary. Good decision making requires three things: intellect, experience, and enough time.

> *The essence of the ultimate decision remains impenetrable to the observer—often, indeed, to the decider himself. There will always be the dark and tangled stretches in the decison-making process— mysterious to even those who may be intimately involved.*
> —John F Kennedy, former U.S. president

Six Thinking Hats

A powerful but simple tool for analyzing alternatives is Edward de Bono's so-called thinking hats. De Bono devised the technique for management teams whereby each member of the team would do a different-colored hat according to their role in the evaluation process. It works just as well for individuals. You can conduct the exercises that follow in your head, but you may find it useful to think with a pen in your hand and to keep a record of your thinking so that you can study and reflect upon the finer points of your analysis at leisure.

- Blue hat: *thinking about thinking* what are you trying to achieve from the process?
- Red hat: *emotion*, how do you feel about the idea? No justification is required here, just raw emotion and intuition.

- White hat: what information do you need to make a decision?
- Black hat: what are the risks, and what is likely to happen in the future?
- Yellow hat: taking a positive view, what is the best possible scenario? Give reasons for your answer.
- Green hat: looking for new ideas and new ways of doing things. Where could I go from here?

It is usually best to start with the blue hat. Donning the blue hat means being clear about what you hope to achieve by thinking about alternatives. It gives clarity to the process; helps you figure out the purpose of the process. For example:

- "I need to decide which of the inspected premises are going to be rented by me."
- "I need to decide whether to continue paying for warehouse space to hold paper records or whether to scan the whole lot into a computer and move to electronic holdings."
- "I need to decide whether to take the offer of voluntary redundancy."
- "I need to decide whether to take up the offer of going into partnership."
- "I need to think about what opportunities there are for expansion."

Jean was happy in her job as a classroom teacher. A friend asked her to go into business with her, running an agency for supply of teachers.

Beginning with the blue hat, Jean decided she would use the technique to help her decide whether to take the opportunity. She then used the red hat to express her feelings about the idea, which were a mixture of excitement and fear. Next, she tried the yellow hat to map out the advantages. They were a multitude of possibilities it would open up. It could be a route out of the classroom and the daily grind of teaching. Jean then applied the black hat to examine the risks and the possible downside. These were uncertainty, loss of pension rights, and possible barriers to re-entering teaching if the venture failed. She also wondered whether she might miss teaching and school life. Jean then applied the green hat to expand the possibilities. "I am happy as a teacher now," said Jean to herself, "but how will I feel in 5 or 10 years' time ground down, stressed out?" Jean then considered another possibility: should she stay in her present job and think about applying for a headship or moving into administration? Jean then applied the white hat and realized that she needed to know more about the idea. For instance, could her friend guarantee a salary and pension?

Applying these hats added clarity to what Jean was being offered, and she decided that she needed more information. These hats will bring clarity to the information regarding a particular choice, and they will force you to justify everything you do, creating more rational and strategic behavior.

Shortcuts

It is not always necessary to use all of the hats. Particular problems require different types of thinking.

The *six thinking hats* tool is not just about avoiding bad decisions. It is about uncovering possibilities in propositions that we might otherwise reject out of hand as negative or too risky. Stephen was a partner in a large firm of surveyors. He was offered early retirement. His initial reaction was negative ("why me?"). Stephen wondered if he were the victim of a sinister conspiracy. After the initial reaction subsided, Stephen realized that he might have been asking the wrong question. That is, instead of saying, "why me?" he might have done some white hat thinking and asked, "How much is it worth?" He might then have donned the yellow hat and tried to compile a list of advantages of being retired. If the list were a short one, then retirement might not be a good idea after all. Alternatively, Stephen might don the green hat and turn a problem into an opportunity.

What could he do in retirement if he had enough money? Stephen eventually decided to retire if, and only if, the financial package offer was adequate for him to do those things he had never before thought about. Yellow hat thinking is also about finding the proverbial silver lining. Even in the most miserable unlooked-for situations, there are possibilities waiting to be uncovered if only we stop to think about them. Indeed, the impetus to becoming an entrepreneur is often forced redundancy. Green hat thinking is expansive. It involves thinking about what could be. Mont Blanc may be best known for their pens, which also double up as status symbols. The company has done some successful green hat thinking; however, in thinking about how to exploit the brand without overexploiting it, it has made successful incursions into selling watches, luxury leather goods, and fragrances. By contrast, some Swiss watchmakers seem to have been slow to don the green hat. It is only recently, for example, that the exclusive brand Patek Philippe has turned its attention seriously to selling watches to women. It has so far not offered the market pens, luxury leather goods, and fragrances, or attempted to exploit the brand in other ways, for example, by linking the name with luxury makes of cars such as Bentley and Ferrari, as other watchmakers have seen fit to essay.

Expanding your branding to new products and collaborating with other brands is prime green hat thinking. These decisions are to be justified and thought through with the other hats. Once that is complete, you can look for more opportunities with the green hat. This endless cycle of looking for opportunities and justifying them creates a rational system of seeing through the wrong choices and working upon the good ones.

Greens and *yellows* are also useful in thinking about what an idea might evolve into. In the early 1960s, Bruce was asked whether he would like to invest in a new type of business, namely, one where instead of being served from behind a counter, shoppers pushed trolleys around and chose items for themselves and then paid at something called a *checkout*. Bruce shook his head. "It'll never catch on," he said. Thus did he turn down the opportunity to become a director of Walmart. The moral of the story: not enough yellow and green hat thinking. Not enough white hat thinking, either. If Bruce had thought about the financial logic underpinning the idea behind this newfangled idea (white hat thinking), he would have realized that this new business model offered potentially powerful economies of scale savings that could be passed back to shoppers. Green hat thinking might have revealed the generative possibilities of the idea, such as the attraction of having many products under one roof. Yellow hat thinking might have helped him to foresee the possibilities of *cloning* and all that that implied.

Bruce decided in haste and repented at leisure. Some decisions have to be made quickly, but whenever possible, take your time. Time is particularly important in facilitating green hat thinking because it can suggest possibilities that might not be immediately apparent. Sally inherited a clothes shop that made very little money. Her first instinct was to sell it. Then she began to consider the possibilities.

Taking Your Time

The first decision is usually not the best one. This is because there are three "responders" in you. The first is involuntary, which is a reflex action that does not require any thinking; it happens automatically. The second is short, which responds to urgent requests, such as putting out a fire or hitting the buzzer in the buzzer round in a quiz. The third is the long, which involves planning or responding to things that will happen later on, such as a hunter planning a hunt in the noon to ensure he and his family do not go hungry at night or deciding which subject will take college. We are concerned about the short and long responders. When making important decisions, you want to let your long responder take control. Your long responder only takes control if it feels that the decision does not feel urgent. That is why, you should take your time; your long responder is a better decision maker and ultimately the one you want to make decisions with. Be rational; take your time.

Donning the green hat, Sally realized that there was a gap in the market between what licensed sex shops provide and the softer approach offering a frisson of sexual suggestion (with no licence required) and providing a personal service. Sally decided to experiment with mingling shirts, blouses, and underwear with some more imaginative lines and by offering a sympathetic service. The experiment succeeded. Soon, Sally was soon receiving recommendations from far and wide. She says, "put it this way, if somebody's got a wallet and they've got some money in it, I will take it. You know, bottom line: I am in business and I will take it. But I will give them the best service that I can give them. And we get transvestites. Well, guys, obviously what sort of a bra can I put this in? I don't laugh at them. I'm fascinated actually. But I think they come because I say, 'Well, if yer putting them thongs on, where do you tuck your bits?'

Moreover, they say, 'What?!'

But how do you learn if you don't ask?

And they don't get embarrassed because I'm not laughing. I'm genuinely interested in what they do. And then somebody'll say to somebody, 'Go up there. They won't laugh at you, they'll actually help you.'"

Exploring the Snags

According to Edward de Bono, most decisions fail because of insufficient black hat thinking. No matter how tantalizing the opportunity, you should always explore the risks and possible downside.

That said, begin by considering certainties before worrying about risks. For instance, if you buy a north-facing house, no amount of wishful thinking will make the property suddenly jump round and face south. If a business is located 200 km away, that journey is not suddenly going to shrink to 20 km. Immediately you open a business, money will start to flow out. American Express made this mistake when they diversified from issuing charge cards to issuing credit cards. The former were payable at the end of every month and in any case only available to persons meeting rigorous income requirements, whereas the latter involved longer-term loans and were available to lower-income groups. The increased risk was obvious enough, but the company failed to take due account of it and lost money on customer defaults accordingly. Now that we uncovered potential problems, the next question is, can you cope? Be specific: if you are opening a business, where is the money for rent, rates, and so forth to come from? How long can you afford to make those payments? Can you arrange credit facilities for essential supplies? If so, will they be adequate to tide you over until the business becomes established? If some of the rooms in the premises face south, would they suffice for your main needs? These are all questions that need to be answered. They require thought and action. They require data and research. You need to get your numbers right, or you'll be in the red.

Emphatically, the existence of risks and problems need not be a reason to reject an opportunity. The question is whether you can de-risk the venture or take counter-measures. Richard might have prospered if he had taken an experienced solicitor into partnership with him or entered into a consultancy arrangement. The brewery might have survived as an independent entity if the management team had opted for a modest increase of production instead of reaching out for a huge upsurge. The brewery's managers neglected to ask important questions such as how they were going to sell all the beer they produced and how they would finance upfront payments due to customs and excise.

Cash flow is essential. You want as much as you can have to come in, but the least amount going out. There are essential things, like rent for a building, which will drain your cash. Some things are not that important, such as having bulletproof windows (assuming you work in a safe neighborhood). There are small costs and big ones; the big ones are your focus.

De-risking ventures also require a financial system to record and access data about financial transactions easily. One way to do this is to create a register for every single thing bought, sold, or thrown away in a register. This recordkeeping can come in handy later on when analyzing your business's potential risks, costs, and bestsellers.

Reframe

Is the bottle half full or half empty? The answer depends on how you frame it! Framing refers to mathematically equivalent expressions. What is interesting, however, is that although half-full and half-empty bottles are mathematically equivalent, psychologically they are not. The former expression evokes positive reactions, the latter negative. For instance, if we say that an expensive drug for treating cancer has a 2 percent success rate, the prospects sound much more optimistic than if we say the failure rate is 98 percent. We are, therefore, more likely to question an idea that has a 98 percent chance of failure than one that has a 2 percent chance of success. We might well invest in the latter before we invest in the former! To counter this form of bias, reverse the framing. If a proposition is presented positively, see how it appears when framed negatively and vice-versa.

Reframing can be applied in different ways to put ideas into perspective. Peter had founded a successful business selling camping gear. He was keen to expand. A friend owned a shop in another town. The shop sold second-hand office equipment and was not doing very well. The friend offered to sell some of Peter's camping gear in his shop. The friend suggested splitting the rent 50/50. Peter was excited by the possibility because he saw it as a low-risk opportunity to achieve an important goal. Once he thought about it, however, and reframed the problem, he realized it was also an invitation to pay half of his friend's rent. Peter did reject the idea and instead negotiated a lower rent. In fact, after six months, Peter ended up moving his gear out of the shop as the experiment was clearly not working.

Showstoppers

You can seek for perfection, but you will rarely find it. A form of pragmatic thinking is to consider fitness for purpose. In other words, will it do?

Be careful about making compromises. According to the proverb, half a loaf is better than none. If you are hungry, yes. Otherwise, compromise may be dangerous. It is the difference between an opportunity and a liability.

Imagine opening a sandwich bar. Passing trade is imperative. The only premises available to rent are just round the corner from the high street. You may be tempted to *give it a go*. After all, it is very close to your ideal of the high street. This is not a sensible compromise but a recipe for disaster. You may say, "it will do to get started," or "I have to start somewhere," or "I will never get started." I understand your anguish, but would you take your life savings and burn them? That is precisely what you are being invited to do here because the odds are so heavily against you. By definition, passing trade rarely turns corners; you might as well be trying to sell sandwiches on Mars for all the good it will do. The offer is unfit for purpose, so reject it.

Do not look for the second-best option. To start a successful business, you need all the ingredients. You cannot take an alternative for something imperative to the business; it is essentially throwing away your money. Remember, there is a difference between a high-risk, high-reward strategy and a business destined to fail.

Incidentally, I think this is why many successful entrepreneurs seem arrogant. Show them something or try to sell them an idea and they may respond brashly, "That's no good to me." Successful entrepreneurs know what they need to be successful, and they have the patience and resilience to search for it.

Fact, Not Assumption

It is vital to distinguish between fact and assumption. This may seem obvious, but we make assumptions all the time, and frequently without recognizing the fact. Every time we switch on the kettle, we expect the water to boil, but it is an assumption nevertheless. Every time we board a train, we assume it will take us to the place marked on the destination board, but it is an assumption. As the brewery managers discovered to their cost, an eightfold expansion in beer production did not, as they seem to have tacitly assumed, mean an eightfold expansion in profits. The law of diminishing marginal returns applies.

Crystal and her partner decided to open a Chinese takeaway business. The plan was to convert premises in a row of terraced houses. The premises had previously been a newsagent's. There was a gas tap in the kitchen. This was important, because running a successful takeaway means being able to produce food quickly. Electricity is almost useless for this purpose. It was only when Crystal applied to have the gas reconnected that she discovered the tap was defunct. The gas supply had been permanently disconnected long ago. By then, the pair had invested heavily in converting the premises. Given the presence of the gas tap, it was reasonable to assume a supply of gas to the premises, but it was an assumption nonetheless, and wrong.

One way of differentiating between different types of information is to distinguish between:

- Know for certain
- Unsure
- Assumed

Interestingly, it is the *known* fact that are often the most dangerous category of information because, like the gas tap, when tested, they turn out to be mere assumptions.

Search for the hidden, rather more subtle assumptions. *Keen to Sell* moved their estate agency from a fairly large town to a smaller one just 8 km away. The partners thought it was a low-risk move because they had already built up a substantial business. As they saw it, they were merely swapping offices. Yet, the decision almost bankrupted them. Far from merely relocating, they ended up starting from scratch, and their resources were barely adequate to see them through the initial financially lean phase of re-establishing themselves. No matter how sure you are of something, check to make assurance doubly sure. If Barings had done that, they might still be in existence. Generally speaking, higher profits in investment banking mean higher risks. Yet, the managers of Barings Bank were not in the least bit worried when Nick Leeson's alleged profits began to outstrip those of the entire organization because they knew that Leeson's contracts were matched. Matched contracts mean that a contract with one party to buy was matched with an equal and opposite contract with another party to sell and vice-versa. Peter Norris, Barings' chief executive, who chaired the committee that supposedly monitored Leeson's trading, said, "Discussion started with a reconfirmation that all our positions were fully matched. That premise was never doubted."

The media subsequently speculated that Barings must have known about Leeson's entrepreneurial trading strategy and maybe even conspired with him. In fact, recorded transcripts of conversations between various members of the bank's management point to the complete opposite, that is, Barings felt secure in the knowledge that Leeson's trades were matched. That premise was never doubted even though the bank's future rested upon it, and even though, latterly, markets in the Far East were ablaze with rumors, suggesting that Barings was incurring massive exposure to a mystery customer. It was only when Leeson mysteriously disappeared that Barings examined his accounts and discovered that Leeson's trades were not matched at all. In fact, they were completely open, exposing Barings to catastrophic risk, and Leeson's mystery customer was none other than Barings itself.

This is a very, very important part of critical thinking. Critical thinking and rational decision making are arguably the best tools for a great entrepreneur. You must question all the information you are given. Is there any assumption being made? Is this first-hand or second-hand data?

If it is second-hand, can I trust the source? These are questions that every piece of data must pass. You must not only scrutinize the ideas you get, but you must also scrutinize the data.

Chapter Summary

- The six thinking hats are: Blue hat; what is the aim? Red hat; how do you feel about it? White hat; what information do you need? Black hat; what are the risks? Yellow hat; what is the most optimistic viewpoint? Green hat, how can I improve from here?
- Go through all the modes or *hats* of thinking to apply critical thought to the idea you want to implement.
- For specific problems, you can skip some hats. What matters is putting yourself in the correct *mode* of thinking.
- Delay each decision to the most extended length within reason. The more time you have to think about it, the better and more calculated your decision will be. This does not mean delaying your plans or others' plans to take extra thinking time; it just means if you can sleep on it, definitely do.
- Black hat thinking or risk analysis is usually the most scarce, so be aware of the risks and take an active step to list down all the possible risks in this industry, how you can mitigate them, and if you cannot, what their potential costs are—plan with these risk losses in mind.
- Flip the framing of propositions to see the other side. If something says this works 98 percent of the time, think about the 2 percent.
- Be careful about compromises, they may seem only slightly worse than what you wanted, but they can make the mile of a difference. Never go for second best unless your business can take the hit. If what you want is not available and it is a core component of that business, you must try by all means to get it because, without it, you will be running a soon-to-close shop.
- Be very aware of your assumptions; having assumptions leads to uncertainty, and uncertainty leads to mistakes. Get your info right before you go through with something.

CHAPTER 6

Importance of Business Research in Delivering a Successful Startup

Knowledge is power. It is the ultimate tool. Research helps attain knowledge much before it is supposed to be used. That makes it a valuable asset. Researching is vital to know your consumers, suppliers, and, more importantly, the business and industry itself. Without research, you are risking money blindly.

The best way to live is to live like you know nothing; this is the only true wisdom.

—Socrates

Chris, who lives in New York, was on the lookout for new business opportunities; he looked around the city and realized that most stores did not sell budget-friendly tablewares. Two of the local retailers in the city sold expensive high-end items; however, none of the two sold what was readily needed by the people daily. After a while, Chris decided to open his store and sell high-end tableware for a low price. What happened here was that Chris spent thousands of money on creating a new line while also spending an additional thousand more to bring his shop to match the new product line. After all of this effort, the sad occurrence was that it took Chris over a year before realizing that there was no immediate need for his new product line in his city.

Unfortunately, proper research into the area or city would have helped Chris to know that the place was flooded by retirees, all of whom do not have an immediate need for new tableware. If he had done enough research into the community and knew the type of people living in this particular area, he would have long known all that matters to the success of those competitors in the area. However, it was unfortunate that he had sunk even before he could learn to swim.

The irony of this story is that the shop owner could easily have avoided his loss if he had first acquired some basic information before spending his money. Instead, he relied on an uninformed hunch, an unchecked desire to branch into a new area, and a misplaced notion of local buying habits.

Step One: How to Build a Strong Foundation

Whether a business idea involves selling a copycat product (or service) or selling something unique, there are only two reasons why an entrepreneur should undertake the time, effort, and expense of creating a new business to introduce it: (1) customers have shown that they want it and (2) there is sufficient enough demand for the proposed product to make a profit. Successful enterprises sell what customers want to buy rather than what the entrepreneur wants to sell. Period. How does an entrepreneur find out what customers want to buy? Research. The more research that's conducted in business, the less risk is taken. Equally important is that the investment costs behind a product or service should relate directly to the amount of research performed. For example, a restaurant does not have to conduct an expensive, full-scale study to determine its next menu item. On the other hand, a new restaurant facing expensive equipment and raw material purchases coupled with employee training costs and other investments in time and money will require more scrutiny. Why? Consider this statistic: on average, out of every 100 proposed new product ideas conceived by manufacturers, 39 begin the development process, 17 survive it, and eight reach the marketplace. However, incredibly, only one product achieves the objectives behind introducing it first (making money).

Before you venture into a new business, it is essential to research why most failed products do not achieve their aims or objectives. Read further to find out the reasons behind most failures:

- The potential market was poorly studied and overestimated.
- The product was improperly positioned in the market.
- Competitors fought back harder than anticipated.

- A *me too* type of product was offered, which was no different from the competition.
- A poorly designed product.
- The production costs were way higher than the budget restriction allowed.
- The product was perceived to be too expensive by the public.

On the contrary, products would genuinely tend to produce a profit when:

- An adequately defined concept is initiated before launching to analyze the market profoundly. In this case, customers' needs are met while also ensuring the benefits of the products or services are clearly stated.
- The new product line comes with unmatched quality and is profoundly superior to that of its competitions.
- A successful merger between technology and customer needs is made.
- All stages of a successful product launch are addressed (customer needs are determined, the product is well designed and thought through, extensive tests are conducted to ensure that its intended customers will purchase the product, development needs are met, a cost analysis proves profitability, production methods are found to be sustainable, delivery times and targets are feasible, and the product is well marketed).

The Meaning of Market Research

The word market is defined as a collection of buyers (or potential buyers) of a particular product or service. The purpose of market research, therefore, is to gather information about a product and its demand. Knowing the size and makeup of a market is a good indicator of how potentially lucrative a product might be. As the owner of X-Pak S.A., in Verviers, Belgium, says, "there is no end of finding new ways to make life easier, innovate existing products, improve a service, or sell something. Good research will help you do all of these things. Research can determine if a product idea has profit potential and if demand will sustain a steady income." Additionally, thorough research into a new line of product or business would help to:

- Shed more light into a new product idea with the inclusion of its costs and target market
- Shed more light on selling the product and projecting the possible amount of the product people will buy
- Determine the most suitable price at which the product will be sold
- Determine the most suitable location for the sales of the product
- Make sure the potential entrepreneurs can speak fluently and confidently about the product
- Connect quickly and seamlessly with the paying public
- Reveal information about the size and abilities of the competition
- Discover ways to modify the product or service to maximize its potential
- Explore the demographic makeup of a potential customer base
- Determine if it is time to let go of a wrong idea and find another one

What Are the Objectives of Market Research?

When questioned on how he succeeds so much in his business dealings, Simon Windsor, the now-retired former owner and founder of the Ultra-Force Group worldwide recruitment firm (based in the UK), said, "The absence of evidence is not necessarily the evidence of absence. So I am usually very sure before I invest in the unknown." To help you better understand the unknown, Simon gave several suggestions to spare head every market research project for a new business. They are listed as follows:

1. Determine an accurate estimate of costs.
2. Produce a reliable estimate of revenues.

A good example is when an entrepreneur decides to venture into selling ice cream; he or she must know some basic things before starting:

(a) How much it costs to sell ice cream (including equipment, raw materials, licenses, etc.)
(b) How many scoops of ice cream will have to be sold per week to cover costs

Research into the answers behind these objectives should:

(a) Identify who is going to buy the product
(b) Determine how many are going to buy it
(c) Provide a reasonable estimation of how long the demand will allow for the product to last

What Are the Required Tools Needed to Conduct Market Research?

Market Research, a Four-Stage Procedure

1. During the first stage, a question or opportunity is defined regarding the entrepreneur's product wishes to introduce. (For example, can the local market support a new ice cream parlor?)
2. In the second stage of research, the entrepreneur must decide on the tools he or she will use to obtain the necessary data (e.g., surveys, demographic studies, income analysis, etc.).
3. The collection of information occurs in the third stage.
4. The fourth stage analyzes all information that has been gathered.

Two Types of Data Tools Fulfill the Second Stage

- Primary data consists of obtaining information firsthand, at its source, for a specific purpose. Primary data collection methods include questionnaires, personal interviews, interviews with groups of people (focus groups), and mail and telephone surveys.
- Secondary data involves information that has already been collected, usually for another purpose. Examples include

demographic studies, surveys, college and university research projects, magazines, books, government data, Internet searches, and so on. Secondary information can also be found in libraries, small business administration (SBA) offices, the Service Corps of Retired Executives (SCORE), local Small Business Development Centers (SBDC), local enterprise councils, a Chamber of Commerce, or even a community bank. Careful Internet searches can also be invaluable.

The Source of Secondary Data Collection

The advantage of getting secondary data is that it does not take so much time because it has already been collected. You can get secondary data through:

Books. Examples include:

- The Business Periodical Index, which lists business articles that appear in major business publications
- The Encyclopedia of Associations, which lists and describes organizations and groups across the United States
- Standard & Poor's Industry Surveys, which provide statistics and analyses of industries

Commercial information (usually sold to subscribers). Examples include:

- The A.C. Nielsen Company provides data on market share, retail prices, sales, television audiences, household purchases, and much more.
- Information Resources, Inc. collects supermarket scanner information, grocery product movement data, and customer behavior.
- NFO Research provides information for mail order businesses, the beverage industry, product testing, attitude and usage studies, tracking, and market segmentation.
- Simmons Market Research Group (MRB Group) publishes an annual report on lifestyles and regional demographics in regards to age, sex, income, and brand preference.

International data sources. Examples include:

- The Asian Economic Handbook
- Country studies
- The Demographic Yearbook (information on 220 countries published by the United Nations (UN))
- The Economic Survey of Europe
- The Europa Yearbook
- The Statistical Yearbook (UN)
- International Financial Statistics
- International Marketing Data and Statistics
- The International Trade Statistics Yearbook (published by the UN)

Periodical titles. Examples include:

- *Advertising Age*
- *The Journal of Marketing Research*
- *Marketing Week*
- *The Journal of Consumer Research*
- *The Journal of Marketing*
- *Chain Store Age*
- *International Journal of Research in Marketing*
- *Sales and Marketing Management*
- *The Progressive Grocer*

The Source of Primary Data Collection

Make no mistake; primary data requires courage, time, and effort to collect. Questions must be proposed and written down, the right people need to be approached, and answers must be analyzed unbiasedly. Do not be afraid to ask for help. Knowledgeable people who have been through this process before will significantly add to the validity of research results. Examples of primary data collection include:

1. **Observing the behavior of people.**
   - Posing as a customer to see what a competitor is doing
   - Counting the number of customers that walk into a similar business or stop in front of a display

- Showing preliminary ads or samples to customers in order to gauge their reaction
- Investigating vehicular traffic flow patterns and the location of competitors

2. **Telephone interviewing**

Phoning potential interviewees is a fast, efficient way to speak to large numbers of people. Numbers from neighborhood or membership phone books can provide a rich source of contacts because people of similar income brackets usually cluster in the same area. The drawback to phone interviews is that many people use answering machines to screen their calls and are offended by unsolicited phone calls (especially during mealtimes). Another obstacle to phone interviewing is that mobile phone numbers can be challenging to obtain.

3. **Group interviews (creating focus groups)**

Bringing some people together (or visiting a group or club that meets regularly) can be a convenient way to gather opinions, explore issues, and probe for information. A good focus group can also act as a brainstorming session, in that the input of different people working together usually produces more than what one individual can provide on his or her own. Drawbacks include pre-existing groups may not paint an accurate picture of the community as a whole, groups can be harder to control than one-on-one interviews (individual voices may not be heard in a group), and some groups may expect payment in return time.

4. **Questionnaires**

A questionnaire is a written set of questions designed to obtain and focus a targeted participant's response (which is harder to do than it sounds). Questionnaires can contain open-ended questions (in which the respondent provides a short answer) or closed-ended questions (in which the answers are already written, and the respondent chooses the most appropriate response). Each has its advantages and disadvantages. Close-ended questions can be answered easily and quickly, but they do not allow for unforeseen options because their answers are limited. Open-ended questions can reveal more than closed-ended questions but can turn people off if they are too personal or require long answers. Whether open or closed, questions should be simple, clear, concise, and purpose-driven. Do not be afraid to play around with questions if they do not produce meaningful responses. Most people who use questionnaires learn as they go.

Never Walk Away From Giving Hardwork and Time to Your Business Research

As stated at the beginning of this chapter, the point behind the research is to reduce risk. The more money a business needs to get off the ground, the more proof is needed to ensure that the investment behind it is a wise one. When conducting research, do not talk to a half dozen friends and family members, then send out a few questionnaires and consider the task complete. Remember that research is the best way to obtain an estimate of future sales. This can be accomplished in part by exploring the demographic trends listed in the public records of local city halls (e.g., is the population of the type of people who will buy your product going up or down?). Lastly, always keep in mind that market research is not a perfect science because buying behavior is notoriously difficult to pin down.

Therefore, as markets tend to change rapidly, different research sources and methods should be used to confirm results—a process called triangulation. In other words, combine at least one or more primary and secondary approaches before establishing a conclusion.

Develop a clear, written vision of what type of service or product you want to sell—then refine it with research. Scottish entrepreneur Michelle Mone, the creator of the Ultimo lingerie line (and founder of MJM International), spent three-and-a-half years researching the design and tailoring of her famous bra before hitting upon a style and shape that satisfied her intended customers. She became a leader in her chosen field, thanks to her research before going into business.

Know your true intentions and why you want to start a business—good research questions will flow from knowing precisely what you want to do and why.

Learn to describe your business (or product) and its benefits in less than 30 seconds. Doing so will enable you to converse with people without boring them—and it will provide more time for the people, you are questioning to speak their minds.

Conduct as much of your research as possible. This does not mean that you should not ask for help. It means that since you are responsible for your business, you should be deeply involved in all aspects of the research process.

Carry out a pilot study before undertaking a significant research project. A pilot study tests research questions and methods against a dozen or so people to determine if the questions asked in a questionnaire and the way they are presented thorough and appropriate.

Do not ignore the competition. When conducting research, find out what potential customers think about your competitors.

Investigate the costs of producing your product as you explore the potential market. Costs must always be weighed against profit potential before a business can be deemed viable.

Do not forget to factor in insurance needs when researching cost estimates.

Chapter Summary

- The research of an industry before entering it is crucial, and it is necessary because, without it, you will invest in things with no or negative returns, unbeknownst to the danger you are buying into.
- Successful businesses sell what the consumers want, not what the entrepreneur wants to sell. Look for market signals such as high margins, low number of firms, or recent privatization/fall of a large firm. Opportunity comes from the ashes of loss.
- Be aware of the understanding of failures; many of the main reasons include wrong overall product, lousy timing, and poor financial planning.

- Market research aims to produce estimates on costs and revenues by analyzing the current demand situation of the market, the current state of competition and your potential competitors, and the substitutes and makeup of the product you will be selling.
- Your objectives should be finding out: who is buying the product, how many, and for how long.
- Stages: (1) Identify key questions and objectives. (2) Decide on tools for research. (3) Collect information. (4) Organize and analyze.
- There are many sources for primary and secondary data collection; it is suggested you try to keep your sources mainly from primary and from as many sources as possible.
- Never walk away from hard work; nothing is for free. As Andy Dufrense from *The Shawshank Redemption* said, "It comes down to a simple choice. Get busy living or get busy dying."

CHAPTER 7

Finding the Right Name for Your Business

A name is essential. It is the first thing a customer will hear about your business, and it is the tag placed on all your efforts and ventures in the enterprise. It is the foundation for your marketing and branding, and different kinds of names can bring in or deter different sorts of customers. The name of your business will be on your products, and everywhere your company has a presence, so choose wisely.

What is in a name? A lot when it comes to small business success. The right name can make your company the talk of the town; the wrong one can doom it to obscurity and failure. If you are smart, you will put just as much effort into naming your business as you did into coming up with your idea, writing your business plan, and selecting a market and location. Ideally, your name should convey the expertise, value, and uniqueness of the product or service you have developed.

Finding a good business name is more complex than ever. Many of the best names have already been trademarked. However, with advertising costs and competition on the rise, a good name is crucial to creating a memorable business image. In short, the name you choose can make or break your business. There is much controversy over what makes a good business name. Some experts believe that the best names are abstract, a blank slate upon which to create an image. Others think that names should be informative, so customers know immediately what your business is. Some believe that coined names (names that come from made-up words) are more memorable than names that use actual words. Others think most coined names are forgettable. In reality, any name can be effective if the appropriate marketing strategy backs it.

Help From Experts

Given all the considerations that go into a good company name, shouldn't you consult an expert, especially if you are in a field in which your company name will be visible and may influence the success of your business? Moreover, isn't it easier to enlist the help of a naming professional? Yes. Just as an accountant will do a better job with your taxes and an ad agency will do a better job with your ad campaign, a naming firm will be more adept at naming your firm than you will. Naming firms have elaborate systems for creating new names, and they know their way around the trademark laws. They have the expertise to advise you against bad name choices and explain why others are good. A name consultant will take this perplexing task off your hands—and do a fabulous job for you in the process.

The downside is cost. A professional naming firm may charge from 5,000 to 80,000 dollars to develop a name, which usually includes other identity work and graphic design as part of the package, according to Laurel Sutton, a principal with Catchword Brand Name Development. A Google search turned up several companies that charge as little as 49 dollars just for the naming work, but the benefit of using professionals is that spending the money now can save you money in the end. Professional namers may find a better name, which is so recognizable and memorable; it will pay for itself in the long run. They have the expertise to help you avoid legal hassles with trademarks and registration, problems that can cost you plenty if you end up choosing a name that already belongs to someone else. Furthermore, they are familiar with design elements, such as how a potential name might work on a sign or stationery.

If you can spare the money from your start-up budget, professional help could be a solid investment. After all, the name you choose now will affect your marketing plans for the duration of your business. If you are like most business owners, though, the responsibility for thinking up a name will be all your own. The good news: by following the same basic steps professional namers use, you can develop a meaningful moniker that works without breaking the bank.

What Is the Meaning of the Business Name?

Start by deciding what you want your name to communicate. To be most effective, your company name should reinforce the key elements of your business. Your work in developing a niche and a mission statement will help you pinpoint the elements you want to emphasize in your name.

Consider retail as an example. In retailing, the market is so segmented that a name must quickly convey what the customer is going after. For example, if it is a warehouse store, it has to convey that impression. If it is an upscale store selling high-quality foods, it has to convey that impression. The name combined with the logo is significant in doing that. So, the first and most crucial step in choosing a name is deciding what your business is.

Should your name be meaningful? Most experts say yes. The more your name communicates to consumers, the less effort you must exert to explain it. According to naming experts, name developers should prioritize actual words or combinations of words over fabricated words. People prefer words they can relate to and understand. That is why, professional namers universally condemn strings of numbers or initials as a wrong choice. On the other hand, a name can be too meaningful. Naming experts caution that business owners need to beware of names that are too narrowly defined.

Common pitfalls are geographic names or generic names. Take the name *San Pablo Disk Drives* as a hypothetical example. What if the company wants to expand beyond the city of San Pablo, California? What meaning will that name have for consumers in Chicago or Pittsburgh? Moreover, what if the company diversifies beyond disk drives into software or computer instruction manuals? Specific names make sense if you intend to stay in a narrow niche forever. If you have any ambitions of growing or expanding, however, you should find a name that is broad enough to accommodate your growth. How can a name be both meaningful and broad? There is a distinction between descriptive names (like San Pablo Disk Drives) and suggestive names. Descriptive names tell something concrete about a business, what it does, where it is located, and so on. Suggestive names are more abstract. They focus on what the business is about. Would you like to convey quality? Convenience? Novelty? These are the kinds of qualities that a suggestive name can express. Consider the name *Italiatour*, a name developed by one naming company to help promote package tours to Italy. Though it is not an accurate word, the name *Italiatour* is meaningful. Right away, you recognize what is being offered.

Nevertheless, even better, the name *Italiatour* evokes the excitement of foreign travel. It would have been a very different name if it had been called *Italy-tour*. The naming company took a foreign word, *Italia*, but one that was very familiar and emotional and exciting to English speakers and combined it with the English word *tour*. The result is easy to say; it is unique, and it is unintimidating, but it still has an Italian flavor.

Before you start thinking up names for your new business, try to define the qualities that you want your business to be identified with. If you start a hearth-baked bread shop, you might want a name that conveys freshness, warmth, and a homespun atmosphere. Immediately, you can see that names like *Kathy's Bread Shop* or *Arlington Breads* would communicate none of these qualities. However, consider the name *Open Hearth Bread*. The bread sounds homemade, hot, and just out of the oven. Moreover, if you diversified your product line, you could alter the name to *Open Hearth Bakery*. This change would enable you to hold on to your suggestive name without totally mystifying your established clientele.

The Process of Coming Up With the Name

When almost every existing word in the language has been trademarked, the option of coining a name is becoming more popular. Perhaps the best-coined names come from professional naming firms. Some examples are Acura and Compaq, names coined by NameLab. Since its beginning, NameLab has been a champion of the coined name. According to company president Michael Barr, coined names can be more meaningful than existing words. For example, take the name *Acura*: although it has no dictionary definition, it suggests precision engineering, just as the company intended. How can that be? NameLab's team created the name *Acura* from *Acu*, a word segment that means *precise* in many languages. By working with meaningful word segments (what linguists call morphemes) like *Acu*, Barr says that the company produces new words that are both meaningful and unique.

"The naming process needs a creative approach," says Barr. He says that conventional words may not express the innovation or new ideas behind a new company or product. However, a new or *coined* word may be a better way to express that newness. Barr admits, however, that new words are not the right solution for every situation. New words are complex and may create a perception that the product, service, or company is complex, which may not be accurate. Plus, naming beginners might find this coining beyond their capabilities.

A more straightforward solution is to use new forms or spellings of existing words. For instance, NameLab created the name Compaq when a new computer company came to them, touting its new portable computer. The team thought about the word *compact*, but that word alone would not stand out in major media like *The New York Times* or *The Wall Street Journal*. So, Barr says, the team changed the spelling to Compaq to make it more noticeable.

Brainstorming for Names

Begin brainstorming, looking in dictionaries, books, and magazines to generate ideas. Get friends and relatives to help if you like; the more minds, the merrier. Think of as many workable names as you can during his creative phase. Professional naming firms start with a raw base of 800 to 1,000 names and work from there. You probably do not have time to think of that many, but try to develop at least 10 names that you feel good about. By the time you examine them from all angles, you will eliminate at least half.

The trials you put your names through will vary depending on your concerns. Some considerations are pretty universal. For instance, your name should be easy to pronounce, especially if you plan to rely heavily on print ads or signs. If people cannot pronounce your name, they will avoid saying it. It is that simple.

Moreover, nothing could be counterproductive to a young company than to strangle its potential for word-of-mouth advertising. Other considerations depend on more individual factors. For instance, if you are thinking about marketing your business globally or located in a multi-lingual area, you should make sure that your new name has no negative connotations in other languages. On another note, if your primary means of advertising will be in the telephone directory, you might favor names that are closer to the beginning of the alphabet. Finally, make sure that your name is in no way embarrassing. Put on the mind of a child and tinker with the letters a little. If none of your doodlings makes you snicker, it is probably OK. Naming firm Interbrand advises name seekers to take a close look at their competition: "The primary function of a name is to distinguish your business from others. You have to weigh who is out there already, what type of branding approaches they have taken, and how you can use a name to separate yourself."

Testing the Name

After narrowing the field, say, the average grade-schooler can read four or five memorable, expressive names, you are ready to do a trademark search. Must every name be trademarked? No. Many small businesses do not register their business names. As long as your state government gives you the go-ahead, you may operate under an unregistered business name for as long as you like—assuming, of course, that you are not infringing on anyone else's trade name.

Nevertheless, what if you are? Imagine either of these two scenarios: You are a brand-new manufacturing business just about to ship your first orders. An obscure little company in Ogunquit, Maine, considers the name of your business an infringement on their trademark and engages you in a legal battle that bankrupts your company. Alternatively, envision your business in five years. It is a thriving, growing concern, and you are contemplating expansion. However, just as you are about to launch your franchise program, you learn that a small competitor in Modesto, California, has the same name, rendering your name unusable. To illustrate the risk you run of treading on an existing trademark with your new name, consider this: when NameLab took on the task of renaming a chain of auto parts stores, they uncovered 87,000 names already in existence for stores of this kind. That is why even the smallest businesses should at least consider having their business names screened. You never know where your corner store is going to lead. If running a corner store is all a person will do, there is no need to do a trademark search. However, that local business may become a big business someday if that person has any ambition. Enlisting the help of a trademark attorney or at least a trademark search firm before you decide on a name for your business is highly advisable. After all, the extra money you spend now could save you countless hassles and expenses further down the road. Try to contain your excitement about anyone's name until it has cleared the trademark search: "It can be very demoralizing to lose a name you have been fantasizing about."

The Final Name Analysis

If you are lucky, you will end up with three to five names that pass all your tests. How do you make your final decision? Recall all your initial criteria. Which name best fits your objectives? Which name most accurately describes the company you have in mind? Which name do you like the best? Every company arrives at a final decision in its way. Some entrepreneurs go with their gut or use personal reasons for choosing one name over another. Others are more scientific. Some companies do consumer research or testing with focus groups to see how the names are perceived. Others might decide that their name will be most important seen on the back of a truck, so they have a graphic designer turn the various names into logos to see which works best as a design element.

Use any or all of these criteria. You can do it informally: ask other people's opinions. Doodle an idea of what each name will look like on a sign or business stationery. Read each name aloud, paying attention to how it sounds if you foresee radio advertising or telemarketing in your future.

Say it loud: Professional naming firms devote anywhere from six weeks to six months to the naming process. You probably will not have that much time, but plan to spend at least a few weeks selecting a name. Once your decision is made, start building your enthusiasm for the new name immediately. Your name is your first step toward building a strong company identity, one that should last as long as you are in business.

What to Do and What Not to Do

When choosing a business name, keep the following tips in mind:

- Choose a name that appeals to you and the kind of customers you are trying to attract.
- To get customers to respond to your business on an emotional level, choose a comforting or familiar name that conjures up pleasant memories.
- Do not pick a name that is long or confusing.
- Stay away from cute puns that only you understand.
- Do not use the word "Inc." after your name unless your company is incorporated.
- Do not use the word "Enterprises" after your name; amateurs often use this term.

Chapter Summary

When choosing a business name, keep the following tips in mind:

- Choose a name that appeals to you and the kind of customers you are trying to attract.
- To get customers to respond to your business on an emotional level, choose a comforting or familiar name that conjures up pleasant memories.
- Do not pick a name that is long or confusing.
- Stay away from cute puns that only you understand.
- Do not use the word *Inc.* after your name unless your company is incorporated.
- Do not use the word *Enterprises* after your name; amateurs often use this term.

CHAPTER 8

Asking the Right Questions

Part of the art of white hat thinking is asking the right questions. But how do you know the right questions to ask? Self-help starts with identifying what you don't know. The trouble is, you don't always know what you don't know. Experience teaches, but for the inexperienced, this is where a mentor can be enormously helpful. Failing that, try thinking about what you are likely to meet, and consider the sort of questions that might arise.

For example, imagine that you have opened a successful restaurant or hotel. You then decide you would like to develop a franchised business. Try to think through what steps you would need to take in pursuit of your ambition.

Key Steps to Building a Franchise

Protect trade name as a registered trade mark in the geographic areas you wish to expand (e.g., Germany, India, or South Korea).

- Define features that have made your enterprise successful.
- Consider what methods and standards on design, quality, operations management, and brand you need to teach franchisees.
- Determine what systems you will need to have in place to attract franchisees. For example, if your franchise is a hotel, will you offer a computer-based reservations system to support the entire chain?
- Develop a market concept that offers something new and interesting.
- Determine what fees you will charge and other contractual requirements.

Asking the right questions becomes a habit of mind. Start by searching for the keystone question, that is, the central issue from which other questions flow. Study this list, and it will become obvious that there is more to developing a franchise than merely replicating an existing business in another location. Notice, however, that they all flow from one central question, namely: what is it that you intend to franchise? That is the keystone question.

Reiterating, in the last paragraph, all other questions come from the keystone question. Once the keystone question has been answered, you can answer all the other questions. You can work your way through the questions because you have answered the base one, and the rest is just the details.

Weighing Up Alternatives

A complementary technique for weighing up alternatives is the *even swap method*. The technique works, as Benjamin Franklin observed, by finding where the balance lies by examining the *pros* and *cons* simultaneously. For example, if you are looking at two sets of premises and both face south (an important objective), then on that parameter, there is nothing to choose between them. One has a big garden that could be turned into a car park. The other has outbuildings that could be converted as the business expands. As both facilities are equally important to you, they cancel each other out, so you eliminate them. Keep repeating the process of elimination on all the important parameters until you are left with residual advantages. In other words, what, on balance, remains points to the optimal choice.

Killer Application

You can short-circuit this process by concentrating upon the *killer application*. The phrase refers to the pivotal goal, the one thing that really matters. It is an intelligent shortcut to optimal decision making, provided it is used carefully. The BlackBerry had a sparse on features compared with other personal digital assistants (PDAs). I chose it in preference to numerous other possibilities for one reason and one reason only, namely, the tried-and-tested *push* e-mail service a decision I have never regretted.

The Enigma of Emotion

Supposing you have donned all the hats, weighed up the *pros* and *cons*, and yet you are still undecided? Supposing the *killer application* makes the decision obvious and yet you are unsure? Or, supposing analysis reveals that there is little to choose between the alternatives? Or, supposing that you have made a decision that is logical and rationally defensible but does not feel right?

This is the time to listen to what your emotions are telling you. Revisit your red hat thinking. Emotions are crucial to good judgment because we have to live with the consequences of our decisions.

Elaine runs a consultancy specializing in helping small businesses to market their products and services. She had always wanted to be a magistrate. The selection process was long and searching. Elaine had hardly opened the envelope containing the certificate of appointment from the Lord Chancelor when she began to have doubts. It was partly the time commitment: could she really juggle so many days? Then there was the mandatory training requirement and performance appraisal. That felt like a heavy price to pay for the privilege of being able to use the designatory letters JP (Justice of the Peace). Elaine felt torn. Then she looked at her red hat scribble, which included words like *anger*, and she realized that being a magistrate would impose restrictions upon her freedom. No more riding her bicycle for a few meters on the pavement, and she would forever be required to drive within the speed limit. "If you feel like that now," said her friend Pat, who had been a magistrate for many years, "you probably won't feel any better once you start sitting." Elaine decided it was not for her after all. Andrew owns a software company. He specializes in designing programs to help public service organizations detect fraud and corruption. He was offered the opportunity to tender for a contract in Afghanistan a project connected with suppressing the illegal narcotics trade. Andrew was confronted with a dilemma. Apart from the physical danger, his black hat thinking raised questions about breaking out of his comfort zone. Yet his yellow and green hat thinking were both positive. It would be new experience and could open up new possibilities. White hat thinking was also positive. Andrew carefully and systematically compared the contractual requirements with his own skills and experiences and discovered a near-perfect correlation, so he was confident that he was capable of delivering confidence born of fact, not dreams. He decided to let the red hat have the casting vote. It said, *warm, sunny, exciting, FREEDOM! Free at last!* Revisiting his red hat thinking, Andrew realized that although in practice he would actually have less freedom because he would be working behind a gated compound, his emotions were really telling him that his present business represented something of a rut that he needed to escape from. So, despite his reservations, he took a chance and eventually became an adviser to governments, something that would never have happened if he had remained within his comfort zone.

The point is, when you are making decisions, your head will take you only so far. To make a good decision, you also have to analyze and weigh the possibilities, but you also have to listen to what instinct and raw emotion is telling you. So, if, once you have donned the hats and analyzed your spreadsheets, two options emerge as more or less equal, but one attracts you emotionally more than the other (even if the pull is only very slight), then that is the option to choose, because your emotions are telling you something very important.

Chapter Summary

- A critical aspect of white hat thinking is asking the right questions. Without the right questions, you cannot seek the correct information. Make it a habit.
- All questions derive from the keystone question. Start by identifying the keystone question and move onto other things.
- When you have multiple options to choose from, continually and simultaneously remove all features until you are left with only the most essential advantages.
- One way to make your product succeed is to have total focus on one aspect, to outcompete and stand out in the market because you have a superior feature.
- If none of the techniques of rationality works, it is best to try to use the gut feeling.
- When making decisions, your head will take you only so far. To make a good decision; you have to analyze and listen to your gut or emotions.

CHAPTER 9

Writing Your Business Plan

By this point, you should have carried out the relevant research into the viability of your proposed business, including having examined your market and looking at customers and competition. With all this data to hand and convinced that your company will succeed, you now need to start planning the business properly. The best way to do this is to prepare a business plan, which will prove valuable in securing any necessary funding and helping you run the company after launch. This can be one of the most daunting aspects of starting up a business because so much can ride on it. However, if you approach it carefully and logically and understand each essential element, you will have little to worry about. Read on for a definitive guide to drawing up your business plan and the various types of finance it could help securely.

> *If you fail to plan, you are planning to fail.*
> —Benjamin Franklin

What Is the Need for a Business Plan?

Having a well-researched and logical business plan will get your business off to a good start and keep it on track when it is up and running. In the first instance, unless you have a strong plan, you are unlikely to secure any funds, and your idea could fall at the first hurdle. Your plan will serve as a structured form of communication to your investors, whether it is the government's business link service, the banks, or even family and friends, and it will provide reassurance as well as a means for everyone, yourself include, to measure your business's performance.

A business plan will help you to prioritize what exactly needs to be achieved and by when. Do you need to find premises for your business before you hire staff? Should you be talking to wholesalers before your product has been finished? In the current climate, it is also important to outline what strategy you have in place for getting your business through the recession—perhaps you consider it recession-proof, or you have done your research and have started in a sector where companies are growing, or you have strong measures to control expenditure. The answers will be different for each business, but it certainly helps if they are clear in your mind. "If objectives are flagged up, they are more likely to be achieved," says Tim Berry, President of business planning software company Palo Alto. Using your business plan to prioritize critical tasks, you can also use to plan your cash flow. It is vital to establish just how much you intend to spend and when. Whether it is to buy stock, order uniforms, lease equipment, and so on, your business could stall unless your finances match your requirements at the right moment. Compiling a business plan should be at the top of your *to make* list. If you are in a partnership or part of a potential management team, decide early on who will write the plan, and then the same individual should be assigned the task of making the business stick to it. How far ahead to plan will again depend on your aims and the type of business, but a year, broken down month by month, will be a minimum.

Once you have established responsibility and a timeframe, you need to decide on specific criteria on which your business's success will be determined and how these can be achieved. For instance, it could be hitting a given number of sales by a set date through an aggressive marketing campaign or expanding to three more product lines through extensive market research. Whatever these achievement criteria turn out to be, you need to think hard about them without making too many assumptions. Consider your business failing in two or three years and try to imagine the reasons it might do so.

How to Prepare Data for Your Business Plan

This section will describe the critical data you will need to compile before you start, some of which you will be able to get from your market resea0rch, discussed in the previous chapters.

Get a Legal Structure in Place for Your New Business

While, understandably, the focus of most entrepreneurs is on their *idea*, it is vital that the operational and logistical requirements are not neglected.

For example, decisions regarding whether you intend to trade as a sole trader, partnership, or limited company are significant. Before deciding, enlist the help of a local accountant or your local business link office. Similarly, you should understand and cover issues such as your potential value-added tax (VAT) obligations, registering a trademark or trade name, and drafting employment contracts.

Whether you like figures or not, having a thorough understanding of *the numbers* that will impact your business is crucial to running a successful business, particularly at the planning stage. At the outset, it will be essential to understand:

- Your startup costs
- Your funding requirements
- Your cash flow forecast for the following months

Know Your Start-Up Cost

Your start-up costs include how much it will cost to get your business up and running. What will you need to pay out before the launch date (such as legal and administrative fees that may be involved in registering your company and any marketing, ranging from prelaunch advertising to the design of your logo and stationery)? There is also the cost of renting premises if you are not working from home and any stock or equipment you may need, such as general office and information tecchnology (IT) items, to specialist tools required for your particular business. You will also need to consider how much money you will need during the early months, once you are up and running; this is known as your cash reserve and covers you initially when you are likely to be making a loss. How much your cash reserve will depend on how quickly you can start to bring revenue into the company, so you need to consider carefully how long it will take until you reach the breakeven point and move into profit.

Funding Requirements

To get your business off the ground, you will most likely need financial help to cover some of the start-up costs outlined earlier. Your business plan will be a vital tool for convincing lenders to support your company. So, you will need to have carefully worked out how much money you need to borrow and explain your reasoning behind the figure. It is important to remember that once you have secured finance, it will not be easy going back to ask for more, so you must get it the right first time. Although it is wise not to overestimate how much funding you need, as it is likely investors will react unkindly to such an approach, you need to make sure you do not ask for too little, as this will put much pressure on your company. This is when working out the amount of cash you will need in reserve becomes essential and is likely to reach the break-even point.

Know Your Breakeven Point

Your breakeven point is the critical milestone at which your new company stops making a loss and is about to move into profit once all the additional expenses have been taken into account; estimating as accurately as you can when you reach this point is an expected part of your business plan. Before you can work this out, you need to formulate your start-up costs and monthly running costs, taking into account any repayments on loans, salaries, and so on. You then need to build in your sales projections of how many products, or how much demand you will have for your service, per month. By comparing your projected monthly revenues against your total monthly costs, you should be able to develop a point at which you start to move into profit, that is, your breakeven point. Calculating the breakeven point will give you an excellent idea of the costs involved in your business and the level of sales you will need to generate, which will, in turn, affect your overall business strategy. Once you know how much you need to sell in one month to break even, you can work out from your sales projections how long it will take for your business to reach this point. You can also see in the table the elements of the equation that you need to change to reach the breakeven point sooner if you want to.

Cash Flow Forcast for the Next Month

Estimating the amount and origin of cash coming into your business, together with how much is being paid out and where it is going during any given period, is a vital part of good business management. This is known as a cash flow forecast, and it is also what many lenders or investors will be looking for before they decide to invest in your business. This makes it a crucial part of your business plan. Once your business is established, it is usual to produce cash flow forecasts for a quarter or even a year in advance. However, during the early stages of your business, it is probably wiser to do this more frequently, say a month in advance. When formulating a cash flow forecast, you must not overestimate your incoming cash. You will find it easier to get an accurate indication of your outgoings as you should be able to itemize them, as described earlier. The problem is that you are unlikely to accurately identify how much money will be coming in, as you can only estimate how much business you will generate each month. This means it is vital to tread on the side of caution, keeping your forecast on the conservative side.

Detailed Definition of Consumer's Benefits

Many entrepreneurs fail to articulate the benefits of their new business clearly. As a result, the term *elevator pitch* was introduced into modern lexicons as a proposed solution. An elevator pitch is your idea, supported by your business model, company solution, marketing strategy, and competition, all stated in the length of time it takes for a short elevator ride. This simple idea encourages entrepreneurs to think carefully about their language when describing their new business (particularly technological ones). It also reminds you to remain customer-focused and ensure that you concentrate on describing the benefits.

The Need for a Mentor

Many start-up entrepreneurs are paranoid that their idea will be stolen and behave secretively before launch. Often the idea is closely guarded and only discussed with close confidantes. However, your confidantes (often family or friends) may find it difficult to pose sufficiently rigorous questions because they do not want to offend you or lack the relevant experience or judgment to critically analyze your new venture. Hence, an idea with serious flaws, which could have been rectified early on in the process, can move ahead only for the wheels to come off at the most critical phase. It is highly recommended that you engage an independent mentor or plan reviewer at an early stage. This person can help hone your idea before you present it to financiers or bankers.

The Important Element of Your Business Plan

The business plan should give a concise description of what your company will sell or the service it will offer, the buyers you will be selling to, and how you will be filling a gap in the market by touching on pricing and existing competition. So, it should be prepared to a high standard, be verifiable (meaning that you need to back up your statements with facts), and with no jargon or general position statements. It should offer the reader a combination of clear description and analysis, including a realistic strengths, weaknesses, opportunities, and threats (SWOT) test of each area. This will demonstrate to investors that you are realistic about your company's prospects. So, ensure that you have a full appreciation of the risks and you know how to grab your market share, all of which, of course, should have been covered in your market research. For your benefit as well, it must contain details of how exactly you intend to meet your key objectives and sales forecasts, target dates, and who, apart from yourself, is to be responsible for this.

Then comes the boring, but just as necessary part; a financial analysis that shows clearly how much finance you need and where you plan to source it from, a summary of start-up costs, breakeven point, and cash flow forecast (as described), plus profit and loss and balance sheet projections.

The key to all this will be striking a balance between covering your business in enough detail and keeping the plan clear and to the point, for it to be helpful to refer to time and time again rather than just sitting on a shelf gathering dust once you have begun trading. The key features of your plan are first described as follows in brief and then explained in more detail later in the chapter.

How Long Should Your Business Plan Be?

The length of a business plan depends on individual circumstances. It should be long enough to cover the subject adequately and short enough to maintain interest. Unless your business requires several million dollars of venture capital and is highly complex, the business plan should be no longer than 15 pages. It is recommended that you thread on the side of brevity. If investors are interested, they can always call to ask for additional information.

How It Should Look

The plan should look professional. Ensure there are no grammar or spelling mistakes. Use graphs and charts where appropriate, and titles and subtitles to divide different subject matters. Although the aim is to make the plan look good, avoid expensive stationery, as this could suggest unnecessary waste and extravagance.

The Company

The business plan should detail all the critical aspects of your company, namely, the market and customers, the products/services, the strength of the management team—and if there are any talent gaps, identify how you will fill them. The plan should also explain how products will be made or services provided. Realistic financial projections should be outlined, and you should provide different scenarios for sales, costs, and cash flows for both the long and short term.

What If's and Ways Out

Several possible scenarios should be presented, along with how your company would cope in different situations. These *What if?* questions will show how your business will react to or counter the effects of an unexpected drop in sales or an increase in costs. The business plan should also detail potential exit strategies.

Mission Statement and Executive Summary

The last thing to be written is the first part of the business plan: the executive summary. This is the essential section and summarizes in two pages what you have written in detail in the following 10–15 pages. This is where, among other things, you lay down the company's mission statement, a few sentences encapsulating what the business does for what types of clients, your aims for the company, and what gives it its competitive edge. That is, the mission statement should combine the business's current situation with your aspirations.

As with the central part of the business plan, the executive summary should be written and powerfully persuasive, yet it should balance sales talk with realism to be convincing. It should be no more than 1,000 words and should also state your company's legal status. Both these are discussed in more detail later in the chapter.

Proper Forecasting of Your Sales

Developing your sales forecast is not as complicated as most people imagine. Think of your sales forecast as an educated guess. It requires an excellent working knowledge of your business but is much more of an art than a science. Remember that even if you do not have business training, you can guess your own business's sales better than any expert device, statistical analysis, or mathematical routine. Experience counts more than any other factor.

A business plan should usually project sales by month for the next year and annual sales for the following three years. This does not mean businesses should not plan for a longer term than just three years; it simply means that the detail of monthly forecasts does not pay off beyond a year, except in exceptional cases. It also means that the detail in the yearly forecasts probably does not make sense beyond three years. It does mean, of course, that you still plan your business for five-, 10-, and even 15-year timeframes, but you just do not do it within the detailed context of business plan financials. Break your sales down into manageable parts, and then forecast these different elements. Estimate the figures based on the sales line, month by month, then add up the sales lines and add up the months, presenting your estimate graphically in a table or chart; remember that you still need to explain them. A complete business plan will usually include discussing your sales forecast, sales strategy, sales programs, and related information. The text, tables, and charts together will provide some visual variety and ease of use. Remember to position the tables and charts near the text covering the related topics.

Creating a Sales Strategy

Near the sales forecast, you should describe your sales strategy, which should deal with how and when to close sales prospects, how to compensate salespeople, optimize order processing and database management, and how to maneuver price, delivery, and conditions. It should answer questions such as:

- How will you sell? Through retail, wholesale, discount, mail order, or over the phone, for example.
- Will you maintain a sales force?
- How will you train your salespeople, and how will they be compensated?

Your business plan text should summarize and highlight the numbers you have entered in the sales forecast table. Make sure you discuss essential assumptions in enough detail and that you explain the background sufficiently. Try to anticipate the questions your readers will ask. Include whatever information you think will be relevant and that your readers will need. Details are critical to the implementation, and your business plan should include specific information related to sales programs.

- How is this strategy to be implemented?
- Do you have concrete and specific plans?
- How will implementation be measured?

Business plans are about results, and generating results depends on how specific you are in the plan. For anything related to a sale that is supposed to happen, include it here and list the person responsible, dates required, and budgets. All of this will make your business plan more accurate.

Creating Your SWOT Analysis

SWOT analysis is a method of describing your future company in terms of those factors that will most impact the business. Strengths and weaknesses are internal factors, such as the quality of your product or your management skills. By contrast, opportunities and threats are external factors, which may include the development of a whole new market (opportunity), the arrival of a clutch of new competitors, the impact of the recession (threat), or the eventual economic recovery (opportunity). SWOT is an easy, understandable way of identifying key issues and communicating them to others. To make things even simpler to grasp, the typical SWOT analysis is done on a four-cell grid.

Sometimes it helps to start without the grid and list any issues that might affect the business, internal or external, real or perceived. Then, when the flow starts to dry up, organize the chosen items into the SWOT categories. Here is a guide to help you complete the categories.

Strengths

In the first box, list all the strengths of your company:

- Why should you succeed?
- What will you do well?
- Why will customers do business with you?
- What distinct advantages does your company offer?

The critical consideration is honesty. Avoid being too modest or too optimistic. Any SWOT analysis is subjective, but try for a third-party viewpoint: what strengths does the outsider see? A jump-start trick, especially for a group SWOT session, is to begin by brainstorming adjectives that characterize your business, writing them down as quickly as people say them, and then using those words to construct a more considered profile of your company's strengths. If you are the sole proprietor or the prime mover in the business, try starting with a list of your own optimistic personal characteristics.

Weaknesses

A weakness is something that could seriously impede your company's performance, a limitation or deficiency in resources, skills, or capabilities.

These could be factors that you will be able to address on launch. For example, a weakness could be a lack of awareness in the marketplace compared with your competition, which means you will need to promote your company heavily to raise its profile, ideally before launching the business or immediately after. Also, although you may list your knowledge of the market as a strength, the fact that the company will initially be heavily reliant on you could be seen as a weakness. If you can spot the fundamental weaknesses of your proposed venture now, you can address them in time for the launch, and it shows investors that all-important element of realism in your approach. So, do not try to disguise weaknesses; simply acknowledge them and ensure you have a strategy in place to tackle them.

Opportunities

Under opportunities, think about where the openings are for your business or the customer needs not being met by your competitors. You will probably start with marketing issues, presumably because your business fills a niche or can compete effectively, but do include all the possibilities. For instance, think of the exciting trends in your business sector; in terms of markets and technology changes, the legislative and regulatory environment, and social patterns.

Threats

Threats are key impediments that your company will face on launch. What are the more apparent obstacles in your way, both actual and potential? Obvious candidates would include the economic downturn, a sudden rush of bad debts, or a slack sales period leading to cashflow problems. However, try to think further than that:

- What is your competition doing that could take business away from you or stunt your company's growth?
- How might your competitors react to any moves you make?
- What trends do you see that could wipe you out or make your service or product obsolete?

- Might technology changes threaten your products or services?
- What happens if a key customer goes under before paying a sizeable invoice?

It is essential to include a couple of worst-case scenarios. Weighing threats against opportunities is not a reason to indulge in pessimism but rather a question of considering how possible damage may be overcome, bypassed, or restricted.

Having written your business plan, you must find educated people to help you go through it before pitching it to investors. This will help you correct any mistakes and prepare you for questioning.

Chapter Summary

- A business plan is your guiding light, a document of your strategy. Make it well and follow it religiously.
- Understanding the legal structure, the start-up costs, and the requirements to get funding is essential and a part of the basic information needed to craft your plan.
- Your breakeven point, your cash flow forecast, and benefits to the consumer are also essential aspects you must explore and answer before you decide to move on with making your plan. A mentor would greatly help in this process; it is highly recommended that you get one.
- Remember, your plan will be presented to investors, so keep it concise. Most business plans will only require 15 pages, while highly high capital or complex businesses may require more.
- A SWOT analysis lists out the strengths, weaknesses, opportunities, and threats. This is a straightforward method of breaking down a complex industry or system into something manageable and presentable.

PART II

Okay, so we have finished the easy bit. Now for the hard part.

Around 90 percent of the startups fail in their first year, mainly due to bad timing and other problems such as impaired decision making.

That is a scary statistic, but most entrepreneurs only prepare for starting a startup, and they push aside the most significant bit: keeping it alive and profitable. Profitability will not come overnight; it took Facebook two years to get into the green.

This chapter will help you learn the skills necessary to keep a business alive. Although this will not contain everything, it will be enough to get you started on the journey, and from there, you can learn by yourself.

We will be discussing a wide array of things, from how to keep your business environment professional to avoid traps and biases that can poison your decision-making skills.

Good luck; I hope you can make it.

CHAPTER 10

Sourcing for Finance

Money. This is usually where the real differentiation between a living and a slow startup. Irrespective of the quality and potential of the business idea and the business plan's effectiveness, money is what brings that idea to life. Getting money is not hard if you have an excellent idea and an even better business plan, and profit-making potential. In this chapter, we will talk about the sources of getting money and how to to get it.

Some businesses require little more than pocket change to get started; others need hundreds of thousands of dollars or more. Whatever amount is needed, bear in mind that raising money is meant to be a complex process. The obstacles and problems inherent in obtaining money, particularly from a lending institution, are designed to filter out unfit to survive. Put another way, if an entrepreneur fails to raise enough cash to get his or her ideas off the ground, then he or she has shown a lack of what it takes to run a business. There is nothing new in this. "Starting a business is easy," says the owner and operator of Procontra P/L, a building maintenance company in Sydney, Australia, "running it and funding it is hard." Welcome to the world of commercial enterprise, where after 50 doors have been slammed in your face, the next one must still be approached with courtesy, optimism, and a smile.

Sources of Finance

The trick to finding capital, say some entrepreneurs, is getting it from suitable sources and in the correct sequence as a business grows and evolves. This means that when searching for funding, every available avenue should be explored. Learn from every approach. For example, if a loan officer at a local bank turns down your request, politely ask why and use what is said to improve the next pitch. It is often not what a money lender is told but what the moneylender wants to hear that is most important. Furthermore, when looking for lenders, try to find ones specializing in the specific industry or field in which the proposed business is located. Investors are usually more receptive to industries and businesses they understand.

Following, in alphabetical order, are the most common examples of where money can be obtained. Ask around and investigate to determine how each option in your region or country can be maximized.

Banks

Winning over a bank is one of the most challenging hurdles a start-up business faces. Banks are necessary to small business operators for two reasons: (1) they are a safe place to store money and (2) they can be a source of finance and other services. Unfortunately, most banks enjoy loaning money to people and businesses that do not need it. This is because every bank wants to ensure that it gets its money back.

Note also that:

- Banks are, by nature, cautious. Requests for money must, therefore, be backed up with firm facts and figures.
- Banks seek security in the form of proven cash revenues or collateral. If you do not have one or the other, you probably will not get a loan.
- If a bank is uncooperative or uninterested in your needs, move on to another one.
- Banks do not exist to help keep businesses afloat.
- People run banks. If you get to know these people, your chances of success may increase.
- Banks hate surprises. Therefore, if you manage to secure a loan and cannot make a payment on time, you should tell your bank in advance.
- Banks make mistakes. A study in the UK discovered that up to 20 percent of the statements banks send out are inaccurate. It is, therefore, prudent to regularly check bank statements.

- Always approach a bank or banker having done a bit of homework. It shows that you are on top of things, which demonstrates integrity and professionalism.
- Most banks are often open to negotiation when it comes to interest rates. Do not be afraid to haggle.

The Corporate Venturing Approach

Some companies loan money to entrepreneurs in the hopes of establishing a working relationship with them. This is called corporate venturing. The skill or product of the entrepreneur must be of benefit to the company being asked and be backed by a solid business plan. The company to which the idea is being pitched may also seek some equity share (ownership) agreement. Just make sure a patent or copyright first protects the idea or product being pushed.

The Crowdfunding Approach

The practice of obtaining funds by publically asking for small donations has been practiced for centuries. The cost of the Statue of Liberty, for example, was crowdfunded by a newspaper campaign.

Paying for upcoming military campaigns by selling war bonds and writers collecting cash from future buyers to fund an as-yet-to-be-printed book provide two additional examples. Nowadays, more than two dozen crowdfunding sites exist online. These include gofundme, Kickstarter, IndieGoGo, Crowdrise, Patreon, crowdfunding, and so on. Crowdfunding schemes usually involve either pre-selling a product (which is similar to a *production contract* arrangement) or selling some sort of equity in the business producing the product. Either way, it can be challenging to generate the attention of individuals and groups without an established network and skillful media involvement. An extraordinary public relations or marketing campaign (and perfect timing) seems essential to crowdfunding success. Do not be seduced by stories that make crowdfunding look easy. Without first establishing a vibrant business network, crowdfunding can be as fickle and distant as winning the lottery.

Equipment Loan

Expensive equipment (i.e., machinery, display cases, tools, etc.) can sometimes be purchased with an extended, low-interest loan from the company that produces or sells the equipment. In return, the entrepreneur may be asked to sell or advertise the company's products in his or her business (usually via professional signs and displays). Talk with suppliers and manufacturers for more information.

Family and Friends

Entrepreneurs that can prove (or have shown) that they are trustworthy and reliable—and have put together a viable business plan—may be able to find family members or friends who are willing to cough up the cash needed to start a business. Note, however, that these folks should not be rewarded with administrative titles in return for their help (which may create future problems). It is also usually not a good idea to ask friends and family to invest their life savings in business (they may not get it back). As asking friends and family for money is the most personal of routes to take, this avenue must be planned with care and forethought. Infosys founder Narayan Murthy started Infosys with an INR 10,000 (USD 150) loan from his wife in 1981. Today Infosys clocks USD 12 billion in revenue.

Seeking Help From the Government

Local, state, and federal governments sometimes offer financial resources for small businesses if and when specific requirements are met. Examples include businesses that employ disabled people (or minorities), businesses located in need of economic assistance, businesses designed to help the environment, or businesses designed to reduce local problems. Contact a local economic development office for details. A good source for such help in the United States is the book *Free Help from Uncle Sam to Start Your Own Business* by William Alarid and Gustav Berle.

Seeking for Grants

Grants provide money that does not have to be paid back. Universities, professional organizations, governments, and trade associations are typical grant sources (including the European Union—if the business is in Europe). The unemployed, pensioners, young entrepreneurs, artists, and other out-of-the-mainstream groups are usually the most eligible to receive a grant if they qualify—as are competent people trying to set up a business in an underdeveloped area. For the most part, grants do not involve large sums of money—only a few hundred or a few thousand dollars at most—but for a fledgling business, a small amount of cash can go a long way toward reducing expenses. Apart from seed funding, grants can also be obtained for employee training, marketing costs, and insurance.

Do not be ashamed to ask for help in the form of a grant. Just be prepared to fill out lots of forms before and after any money is received.

Shares Issuing

The issuing of shares is a finance option that is only available to businesses that are incorporated.

The advantage of issuing shares is that the people who buy them do not have to pay them back. The disadvantage is that the people who buy shares are part owners of the business, and as such, they can hold the entrepreneur accountable for whatever he or she does (or does not do). Shares can be used in a variety of ways. For example, a cocktail bar in London, England, recently issued shares to its employees as part of its payment package. In return, the bar operator says he has one of the most motivated workforces in the UK.

Small Business Administration Loans

Loans available from the Small Business Administration (SBA) in the United States include:

1. Direct SBA loans (which have a low interest rate). The name comes from the fact that this type of loan is issued directly from the government. Unfortunately, because Direct SBA loans are intended for minorities and veterans, they may be difficult to acquire if the person requesting them does not qualify.
2. Guaranteed loans are sometimes available to individuals whom a bank has turned down. The scheme works by having the government

guarantee a loan (via a participating bank) on behalf of the entrepreneur. More leeway is, therefore, usually given in paying the loan back. For more information on small business administration loans, including tips on raising capital, finding grant resources, equity financing, and more, visit www.sba.gov or contact a local bank or nearby Small Business Development Center.

Soft Loans

Loans are declared *soft* when they do not require security or collateral, their payback schedule is long, and their due dates are extendable. That being said, every penny that is borrowed must be paid back, with interest, just like a regular loan. Small Business Development Centers, local governments, business-oriented banks, corporations, business trusts, and other business-friendly associations are the best places to look for soft loans.

Trade Credit

Some suppliers do not require payment for the merchandise they sell for up to 30 days or longer—so that the purchaser has time to sell the merchandise before paying for it. If a small business has a solid customer base and has little doubt that it can shift merchandise quickly, this can be a creative way to lower inventory costs and begin trading with less money than initially envisioned.

Venture Capitalists

A venture capitalist is a person or group that finances businesses. In return, he or she (as part owner) expects to share in the business's success in which his or her investment has been made while expecting yearly growth rates of up to 40 percent or higher. Because most venture capitalists are successful business people in their own right, they are often adept at determining if a commercial idea is a good one. Note that many venture capitalists are not interested in providing capital for small businesses. Instead, they look for high-flying enterprise ideas with big profit expectations and will pay back their investment very quickly. Additionally, as most venture capitalists are only in it for the money (who is not?), they may sell their shares to unknown buyers in a few years.

Mixing Up the Options

If the sources aforementioned are not enough on their own, consider mixing them up. Maybe a local bank will not lend 100,000 dollars to start a business, but it may consider 25,000 dollars. Additional funds can then be obtained from family and friends, the selling off of personal assets, and so on. Still, more cash can come from grants or through trade credits or equipment loans. Do not be afraid to be creative.

Kristen was setting up the e-commerce business to promote local artisans. She needed 250,000 dollars toward infrastructure cost, marketing, setting up the business, and so on. However, through her savings, she can manage only 50,000 dollars. She wrote an excellent grant proposal to get another 50,000-dollar grant meant for promoting women's entrepreneurship. She presented this idea to a local businessman, and he gave another 100,000 dollars as angel investment instead of 15 percent of the shares of the newly formed company. Kristen arranged the rest of the money through trade credits from the marketing agencies by signing a deal with them to pay after 90 days of the launch. Now Kristen is all set to start her business with a bang.

Chapter Summary

- When in need of finance, shop around, be persistent, and never be afraid to ask for advice.
- Open up every available line of credit before going into business—even if it means taking on more credit cards. Few institutions will loan money to a cash-hungry business after it has been set up.
- Ensure that all equipment and machinery is bought at the best price and under the best conditions. Used equipment may seem like a less expensive alternative to new equipment, but make sure what you buy has lots of life left in it. Entrepreneurs that buy cheap often buy twice. Remanufactured equipment, which comes

with a guaranty, is a much safer bet. (Author note: if you need office furniture, try not to buy brand new items. The cost of new business furniture is usually grossly over-inflated; remanufactured is a far better option, and no one will notice the difference).

- Please get to know your banker before you need money from him or her (i.e., while you are still solvent). Being desperately in need of cash is the wrong time to introduce yourself to a money lender.
- Do your homework before seeking cash. You may need more than you thought. Many entrepreneurs claim that every time they turn around, there seems to be another payment that has to be made (for licenses, fees, duties, permits, etc.). Prepare for this fact.
- Do not let your business die a death from a thousand cuts. Little expenses add up, and they can break a business. Again, factor everything in.
- After you have deduced how much finance your business needs to get up and run, double the figure. (Some entrepreneurs suggest tripling it!)
- The world is littered with failed businesses whose owners were too proud or stubborn to ask for money when it was needed. Borrowing money is not a sign of weakness but rather a normal, everyday business occurrence. Know that taking on debt is often a necessity if you are thinking of expanding.
- Consider selling equity (shares) in your business as a means of reducing debt. Although this means that the people with equity shares will own a part of your business, you do not have to pay them back (which can significantly reduce expenses).
- Lending institutions are more receptive to entrepreneurs that hold production contracts (i.e., orders for a product). Getting potential customers to order a product before your business gets started may be difficult to do, but it can be done. Use such orders to impress a lender.

CHAPTER 11

Legalizing Your Business

Of all the decisions you make when starting a business, probably the most important one relating to taxes is the type of legal structure you select for your company.

Not only will this decision have an impact on how much you pay in taxes, but it will affect the amount of paperwork your business is required to do, the personal liability you face, and your ability to raise money. The most common forms of business are sole proprietorship, partnership, corporation, and S corporation. A more recent development to these business forms is the limited liability company (LLC) and the limited liability partnership (LLP). Because each business form comes with different tax consequences, you will want to choose wisely and choose the structure that most closely matches your business's needs.

If you decide to start your business as a sole proprietorship but later decide to take on partners, you can reorganize as a partnership or other entity. If you do this, be sure you notify the IRS as well as your state tax agency.

Sole Proprietorship

The simplest structure is the sole proprietorship, which usually involves just one individual who owns and operates the enterprise. If you intend to work alone, this structure may be the way to go. The tax aspects of a sole proprietorship are appealing because the expenses and your income from the business are included on your income tax return, Form 1040. Your profits and losses are recorded on a form called Schedule C, which is filed with your 1040. The *bottom line amount* from Schedule C is then transferred to your tax return. This is especially attractive because business losses you suffer may offset the income you have earned from your other sources. As a sole proprietor, you must also file a Schedule SE with

Form 1040. You use Schedule SE to calculate how much self-employment tax you owe. In addition to paying annual self-employment taxes, you must make estimated tax payments if you expect to owe at least 1,000 dollars in federal taxes for the year after deducting your withholding and credits, and your withholding will be less than the smaller of (1) 90 percent of the tax to be shown on your current year tax return or (2) 100 percent of your previous year's tax liability. The federal government permits you to pay estimated taxes in four equal amounts throughout the year on April 15, June, September, and January. With a sole proprietorship, your business earnings are taxed only once, unlike other business structures. Another big plus is that you will have complete control over your business—you make all the decisions.

There are a few disadvantages to consider, however. Selecting the sole proprietorship business structure means you are personally responsible for your company's liabilities. As a result, you are placing your assets at risk, and they could be seized to satisfy a business debt or a legal claim filed against you. Raising money for a sole proprietorship can also be challenging. Banks and other financing sources may be reluctant to make business loans to sole proprietorships. In most cases, you will have to depend on your financing sources, such as savings, home equity, or family loans.

Forming Partnership

If your business is owned and operated by several individuals, you will want to take a look at structuring your business as a partnership. Partnerships come in two varieties: general partnerships and limited partnerships. In a general partnership, the partners manage the company and assume responsibility for the partnership's debts and other obligations. A limited partnership has both general and limited partners. The general partners own and operate the business and assume liability for the partnership, while the limited partners serve as investors only; they have no control over the company and are not subject to the same liabilities as the general partners.

Unless you expect to have many passive investors, limited partnerships are generally not the best choice for a new business because of all the required filings and administrative complexities. If you have two or more partners who want to be actively involved, a general partnership would be much easier to form.

One of the significant advantages of a partnership is the tax treatment it enjoys. A partnership does not pay tax on its income but *passes through* any profits or losses to the individual partners. The partnership must file a tax return (Form 1065) that reports its income and loss to the IRS at tax time. In addition, each partner reports his or her share of income and loss on Schedule K-1 of Form 1065. Personal liability is a significant concern if you use a general partnership to structure your business. Like sole proprietors, general partners are personally liable for the partnership's obligations and debts. Each general partner can act on behalf of the partnership, take out loans, and make decisions that will affect and bind all the partners (if the partnership agreement permits). Keep in mind that partnerships are also more expensive to establish than sole proprietorships because they require more legal and accounting services.

Corporation

The corporate structure is more complex and expensive than most other business structures. A corporation is an independent legal entity, separate from its owners, and as such, it requires complying with more regulations and tax requirements.

The most significant benefit for a business owner who decides to incorporate is the liability protection he or she receives. A corporation's debt is not considered that of its owners, so you are not putting your assets at risk if you organize your business as a corporation. A corporation also can retain some of its profits without the owner paying tax on them.

Another plus is the ability of a corporation to raise money. A corporation can sell a stock, either standard or preferred, to raise funds. Corporations also continue indefinitely, even if one of the shareholders dies, sells the shares, or becomes disabled. The corporate structure, however, comes with several downsides. A major one is higher costs. Corporations are formed under the laws of each state with their own set of regulations. You will probably need the assistance of an attorney to guide you. In addition, because a corporation must follow more complex rules and regulations than a partnership or sole proprietorship, it requires more accounting and tax preparation services.

Another drawback to forming a corporation: owners of the corporation pay a double tax on the business's earnings. Not only are corporations subject to corporate income tax at both the federal and state levels, but any earnings distributed to shareholders in the form of dividends are taxed at individual tax rates on their income tax returns.

One strategy to help soften the blow of double taxation is to pay some money out as salary to you and any other corporate shareholders who work for the company. A corporation is not required to pay tax on earnings paid as reasonable compensation, and it can deduct the payments as a business expense. However, the IRS has limits on what it believes to be reasonable compensation.

S Corporation

The S corporation is more attractive to small-business owners than a regular (or C) corporation. An S corporation has some appealing tax benefits and still provides business owners with liability protection. With an S corporation, income and losses are passed through to shareholders and included on their tax returns. As a result, there is just one level of federal tax to pay.

In addition, owners of S corporations who do not have inventory can use the cash method of accounting, which is more straightforward than the accrual method. Under this method, income is taxable when received, and expenses are deductible when paid.

S corporations can also have up to 100 shareholders. This makes it possible to have more investors and thus attract more capital, tax experts maintain. S corporations do come with some downsides. For example, S corporations are subject to many of the same rules corporations must follow, which means higher legal and tax service costs. They also must file articles of incorporation, hold directors and shareholders meetings, keep corporate minutes, and allow shareholders to vote on major corporate decisions. The legal and accounting costs of setting up an S corporation are also similar to those for a regular corporation.

Another significant difference between a regular corporation and an S corporation is that S corporations can only issue one class of stock. Experts say this can hamper the company's ability to raise capital.

In addition, unlike in a regular corporation, S corporation stock can only be owned by individuals, estates, and certain types of trusts. In 1998, tax-exempt organizations such as qualified pension plans were added to the list. This change provides S corporations with even greater access to capital because several pension plans are willing to invest in closely held small-business stock.

Signing the Papers

To start incorporating, contact the secretary of state or the state office responsible for registering corporations in your state. Ask for instructions, forms, and fee schedules on incorporating.

It is possible to file for incorporation without the help of an attorney by using books and software to guide you. Your expense will be the cost of these resources, the filing fees, and other costs associated with incorporating them into your state.

If you do it yourself, you will save the expense of using a lawyer, which can cost from 500 to 5,000 dollars if you choose a firm that specializes in start-up businesses. The disadvantage is that the process may take you some time to accomplish. There is also a chance you could miss some small but important detail in your state's law.

One of the first steps in the incorporation process is to prepare a certificate or articles of incorporation. Some states provide a printed form for this, which either you or your attorney can complete. The information requested includes the proposed name of the corporation, the purpose of the corporation, the names and addresses of those incorporating, and the location of the corporation's principal office. The corporation will also need a set of bylaws that describe in greater detail than the articles how the corporation will run, including the responsibilities of the company's shareholders, directors, and officers; when stockholder meetings will be held; and other details critical to running the company. Once your articles of incorporation are accepted, the secretary of state's office will send you a certificate of incorporation.

Rules of the Game

Once you are incorporated, be sure to follow the rules of incorporation. If you fail to do so, a court can pierce the corporate veil and hold you and the other business owners personally liable for the business's debts.

It is essential to follow all the rules required by state law. You should keep accurate financial records for the corporation, showing a separation between the corporation's income and expenses and those of the owners.

The corporation should also issue stock, annual file reports, and hold yearly meetings to elect company officers and directors, even if they are the same people as the shareholders. Be sure to keep minutes of shareholders' and directors' meetings. On all references to your business, make sure to identify it as a corporation, using Inc. or Corp., whichever your state requires. You also want to make sure that whomever you will be dealing with, such as your banker or clients, knows that you are an officer of a corporation.

Limited Liability Company

LLs, often referred to as *Lacs*, have been around since 1977, but their popularity among entrepreneurs is a relatively recent phenomenon. An LLC is a hybrid entity, bringing together some of the best features of partnerships and corporations.

LLCs were created to provide business owners with the liability protection that corporations enjoy without double taxation. Earnings and losses pass through to the owners and are included on their tax returns.

Does it sound similar to an S corporation? It is, except that an LLC offers business owners even more attractions than an S corporation. For example, there is no limitation on the number of shareholders an LLC can have, unlike an S corporation, which has a limit of 100 shareholders. In addition, any member or owner of the LLC is allowed a full participatory role in the business's operation; in a limited partnership, on the other hand, partners are not permitted any say in operation.

To set up an LLC, you must file articles of organization with the secretary of state in the state where you intend to do business. Some states also require you to file an operating agreement, which is similar to a partnership agreement. Like partnerships, LLCs do not have perpetual life. Some state statutes stipulate that the company must dissolve after 30 years. Technically, the company dissolves when a member dies, quits, or retires.

If you plan to operate in several states, you must determine how a state will treat an LLC formed in another state. If you decide on an LLC structure, be sure to use the services of an experienced accountant who is familiar with the various rules and regulations of LLCs.

Another recent development is the LLP. With an LLP, the general partners have limited liability. For example, the partners are liable for their malpractice and not that of their partners. This legal form works well for those involved in professional practice, such as physicians.

The Zero Profit Option

What about organizing your venture as a nonprofit corporation? Unlike a for-profit business, a nonprofit may be eligible for certain benefits, such as sales, property, and income tax exemptions at the state level. The IRS points out that while most federal tax-exempt organizations are nonprofit organizations, organizing as a nonprofit at the state level does not automatically exempt you from federal income tax.

Another significant difference between a profit and nonprofit business deals with the treatment of profits. With a for-profit business, the owners and shareholders generally receive the profits. Any left money after the organization has paid its bills is put back into the organization with a nonprofit. Some types of nonprofits can receive contributions that are tax-deductible to the individual who contributes to the organization. Keep in mind that nonprofits are organized to provide some benefit to the public.

Nonprofits are incorporated under the laws of the state in which they are established. To receive federal tax-exempt status, the organization must apply with the IRS. First, you must have an Employer Identification Number (EIN) and then apply for recognition of exemption by filing Form 1023 (Application for Recognition of Exemption Under Section 501(c)(3) of the Internal Revenue Code) or Form 1024 (Application for Recognition of Exemption under Section 501(a)) with the necessary filing fee. Both forms are available online at irs.gov.

The IRS identifies the different types of nonprofit organizations by the tax code they qualify for exempt status. One of the most common forms is 501(c)(3), which is set up to do charitable, educational, scientific, religious, and literary work. This includes a wide range of organizations, from continuing education centers to outpatient clinics and hospitals.

The IRS also mandates that certain activities tax-exempt organizations cannot engage in to keep their exempt status. For example, a section 50l(c)(3) organization cannot intervene in political campaigns.

Remember, nonprofits still have to pay employment taxes, but they may be exempt from paying sales tax in some states. Check with your state to make sure you understand how the nonprofit status is treated in your area. In addition, nonprofits may be hit with unrelated business income tax. This is regular income from a trade or business that is not substantially related to charitable purposes. Any exempt organization under Section 501(a) or Section 529(a) must file Form 990-T (Exempt Organization Business Income Tax Return) if the organization has a gross income of 1,000 dollars or more from an unrelated business and pay tax on the income.

If your nonprofit has revenues of more than 25,000 dollars a year, be sure to file an annual report (Form 990) with the IRS. Form 990-EZ is a shortened version of 990 and is designed for small exempt organizations with less than one million dollars.

Form 990 asks you to provide information on the organization's income, expenses, and staff salaries. You also may have to comply with a similar state requirement. The IRS report must be made available for public review if you use the calendar year as your accounting period file Form 990 by May 15.

For more information on IRS tax-exempt status, download IRS Publication 557 (Tax-Exempt Status for Your Organization) at irs.gov.

Even after you settle on a business structure, remember that the circumstances that make one type of business organization favorable are always subject to changes in the laws. It makes sense to reassess your form of business from time to time to make sure you are using the one that provides the most benefits.

Chapter Summary

- One of the most important decisions you can make is choosing what kind of corporation you want to go for.
- A sole proprietorship has an unlimited liability, which means you may have to pay more than your initial investment, but it gives you absolute control over your firm. Very common in small-scale businesses or family businesses.
- A partnership can be limited or unlimited liability depending on whether you are a general or limited partner. It is also used for small-scale businesses and a few highly skilled professionals collectively running the business; an example would be a clinic.
- A corporation is a limited liability for all owners, but disadvantages include paying more taxes or dealing with more regulations.
- An S corporation is a smaller scale solution for a corporation that limits the number of owners but removes most of the downsides.
- An LLC is a limited liability structure without the downsides of having high taxes but requires some filing work. An LLP is an LLC, but for partnerships, joint in areas of professional work.
- Nonprofit corporations do not have to be charities or such; they can be regular firms; the only difference is that all profit must go back into the business. They are taxed more minor, and they have fewer regulations, but most people will not be willing to invest because their return is zero unless you can persuade them by promoting social entrepreneurship.
- It is highly recommended that you do all legal work through a competent lawyer. If you mess this up right now, it may bite you later down in the line, chomping away a few hundred thousand or even a few billion dollars.

CHAPTER 12

Decisions About Future Investments—The Sunk Cost Trap

The past is the past. If you lose money, do not bias away from a decision just because you did. In the world of business, every decision must have a reason. Accept that you will lose some money at one point in your venture; no one is perfect.

Base decisions on future pay-offs, not past costs. Imagine your broadband connection has failed and you desperately need to restore it. You have been *on hold* on the telephone helpline for five minutes, costing 60p a minute. How long do you continue waiting? Keshav is a part-time stock investor. He invested in few stocks, but due to change in economic conditions, his investments have halved in their value. Should Keshav keep them or sell? Look at another scenario. You are converting an old mill into a block of flats, once buoyant property market has collapsed; should you finish the project?

Being on hold on the telephone, faltering share prices, and a changing market, all of these problems share three features, namely that:

- You have made an investment in anticipation of results
- Results have yet to materialize
- You must decide whether to quit or continue

The dilemma is that if you quit all the time, money, and effort invested in your venture will count for nothing. As with drilling for oil and finding a dry well, your investment has become merely an expense.

Yet, if you persist, you may simply end up making things worse. Supposing the call center does not operate a queuing system; you could be kept waiting indefinitely while costs mount. If shares are in free fall, should you cut your losses immediately?

Sunk Costs

One factor that should not influence such decisions except in special circumstances is the amount already invested in the venture known as past or, as I shall call them, sunk costs. Sunk costs should be ignored because they cannot influence future outcomes. If this suggestion sounds absurdly wasteful, the following simple scenario will illustrate the point.

Say you decide to turn your living room into a corner shop. The conversion costs are 30,000 dollars. The business generates an income of about 200 dollars for a 70-hour week. After two or three years, you begin to tire of the long hours and meager returns. If you closed the shop and took a job stocking supermarket shelves, you could earn 350 dollars for a 40-hour week.

Assuming your goal is to maximize your income and quality of life, you would be 150 dollars a week better off working in the supermarket, and have a lot more free time. Moreover, it becomes obvious that the 30,000 dollars invested in the shop are irrelevant when you reframe the problem as a choice between earning 2.86 dollars per hour in the shop or earning 8.75 dollars per hour in the supermarket.

The Sunk Cost Trap

Intellectually, that decision makes itself. However, research by psychologists suggests that, emotionally, sunk costs can exert a powerful hold.

Part of the problem of letting go of sunk costs is that we become riveted to the past. We become obsessed with what was rather than seeing and acting upon what now is. For instance, if you buy shares at 10 dollars each and the price falls to 80p, you may be unwilling to sell for less than 10 dollars because, as you see it, that is the *correct* price. In other words, the 10 dollars invested becomes the reference point for subsequent decisions.

Researchers who studied bidding prices on the Internet auction site eBay discovered something interesting. They wanted to know whether setting a reserve price is a good idea. By analyzing large amounts of information, they discovered that sellers who dispensed with reserve prices and who started from very low bids tended to achieve higher prices than those who imposed a reserve price. The researchers inferred from their results that starting low without a reserve price creates a *sunk cost* effect as frequent bidding involves investing time and effort. Consequently, as the price of an item rises, early bidders may be reluctant to forgo their sunk costs and therefore become determined to acquire the item at all costs. (The risk with this strategy of course is that if there are few bidders, you may have to sell a valuable item for cheap!)

The eBay research also suggests that it is not just money that counts. We may become psychologically attached to the time and the physical and emotional effort invested. This is Brian's problem. Brian owns a business that makes very little money. Financially, he knows he would be better off closing it down and finding alternative employment. Emotionally, he cannot bring himself to do it because of all that he has invested in the business over the years. He says, "What's holding me here is not being able to let go of the nearly $200,000 that I've put into it. It's very difficult to say goodbye to that, although I know it's gone." This is because it's just not your money; you've put your heart and soul into it.

By contrast, when Sabina's business began losing money, she did the right thing. She said, "I've got jackets which I bought for twenty dollars. I'm selling them for three dollars. It's hard, it's very, very hard."

Hard though it was for Sabina to sell substantially below cost, it is the correct decision from an economic standpoint because it means she can at least salvage something from an unhappy situation. She can use the money to buy new stock that might sell better than the jackets, and can clear space and start again, unlike Brian, who remains shackled by the past. Research has shown, however, that entrepreneurs are more likely to keep businesses they have started themselves even if they are unprofitable, and sell businesses that they have bought, even if they are outperforming the businesses they have started!

It is not difficult to see why entrepreneurs make such decisions. Starting a business involves expending much more time and effort than simply buying a going concern, so the sunk costs are much higher. Economically, however, it is like climbing up an apple tree and ignoring the chainsaw cutting through the bark, at one point, you are going to fall with the tree.

Golden Rule

The golden rule when making decisions involving sunk costs is to focus upon achieving the best possible return on investment for the future. This means seeing the situation not for what it was but for what it has become. What you paid for shares is irrelevant. If the price falls, the reality is that you have 80p multiplied by the number of shares to invest. The question is whether those remaining funds could be invested more profitably elsewhere.

Alan's friend persuaded him to invest 70,000 dollars, which was half his retirement lump sum, in a business venture. The venture failed and Alan's friend then said that his only hope of recouping his 70,000 dollars was to reinvest the remainder of his lump sum in the business. What would you do if you were Alan?

Alan did as the friend suggested and ended up losing another 70,000 dollars. Financially unsophisticated, Alan was unaware that his friend was manipulating *sunk costs* by emphasizing the lost 70,000 dollars, when the economically wise and ethically proper question was whether Alan should take such a huge risk with the remainder of his funds. Given the importance of those funds to Alan, the answer surely had to be *no*.

Waste Not, Want Not?

Imagine choosing between two *TV* dinners. The dinners are identical, and they both have the same *eat by* date. The only difference is that one cost 7.99 dollars, and the other was bought on a special offer for 4.99 dollars. Which of the two dinners would you choose?

Logically, it makes no difference, but when researchers conducted the experiment, they discovered that a significant proportion of diners selected the more expensive meal. We can infer from those results that as human beings, we dislike waste. While waste may be morally abhorrent, our abhorrence can sometimes lead to poor decisions. For instance, research has shown that the more we pay for a theater ticket, the more likely we are to use it. Yet, if it is a poor production, persistence only makes matters worst. Having spent money on the tickets, you then end up paying to travel into town, paying parking costs and, to cap it all, waste an evening. The correct question is: what else could you do with the time and money?

Theater tickets and wasted evenings are one thing. Supposing, however, the decision involves buying a bulk consignment of stock. Some of the items in consignment are unusable and will therefore be wasted. Would you rather take the more expensive option of buying singly? Don't be afraid to *waste* something if it makes economic sense to do so.

Sunk Cost and Success

The sunk costs rule also applies to successful decisions. All else equal, if an opportunity offering a better return upon investment becomes available, we should take it even though it means abandoning a successful course of action.

Anne was lucky. She applied for two jobs and got both. The first job involved attending a two-day assessment center, sitting a battery of tests, and undergoing two searching interviews. It pays 25,000 dollars a year. The second job involved only a 40-minute interview that was really little more than a pleasant chat over tea and biscuits. It pays 35,000 dollars a year. Anne feels that having worked so hard for the first job, she ought to take it. Since, however, all that effort has no bearing on what happens next, all else being equal Anne should reject the first job because the second one offers the best return for the future.

Each decision you make has a hidden cost, which economists call the opportunity cost. It is something that is more than often ignored. Standard accounting of costs and benefits will not help in this; economics will. You must not look only at the best option, but also at the best alternative. What is Anne losing by choosing the first job over the second? She is losing 10,000 dollars a year and potential job satisfaction. If Anne had thought of the offers in this way, she would make a much more rational decision and go for the second one.

This can be applied to business too. Jeremy runs a web development business. His firm makes 100,000 dollars per month, taking up private contracts. One day, a government agency offers him 70,000 dollars for a website that would take a month to build. So, should he take the offer? No. If you look at it from an earnings or accounting perspective, he is gaining 70,000 dollars. However, from an opportunity cost perspective, he is losing 30,000 dollars and potential contracts. When choosing between two of the best alternatives, always consider the opportunity cost.

The Past

Few of us in the western world will ever experience the devastation that war and natural disasters can create. Survivors are left with nothing and have to rebuild their lives as best they can, sometimes having lost literally everything: their home, their livelihood, and their family. Fortunes can be transformed within seconds. The time it takes for a tidal wave to wash in represents the division between the past and the future. What was maybe only a few seconds ago, no longer is.

What is the past is the past. We cannot recall the past five minutes, never mind the past five years. The sooner we recognize this, the better, for if we cling to the past, we risk losing what the future might offer.

Fergus had been a fisherman all his life, as had his father and his father before him. When the fishing industry declined, Fergus promptly accepted the inevitable and converted his fishing boat to take passengers. It was a hard decision because his whole life was invested in the fishing industry. Yet, Fergus is glad that he made the decision, as he now enjoys a second career operating educational and pleasure cruises around the harbor. If Fergus had buried his head in the sand and clung to fishing, he would have gradually gone bankrupt. Then he would have had no money to convert his boat. Besides, someone else might have beaten him to the new business opportunity.

The principle also applies to day-to-day decisions. It is always disappointing when a customer walks away, particularly if you have invested a lot of time and effort trying to achieve a sale. If that happens, respond with charm. Hand the customer your business card and wish them well. Today's sale is lost, but there is always a tomorrow.

Chapter Summary

- The sunk cost fallacy may convince you to invest more in an investment that has proven to be wrong. To avoid this is to ignore all previous investments and take the investment from a fresh perspective. If you were investing in this for your first time, would you?
- This also applies to success. You want to maximize the benefit gained from your time and work, and even if a specific activity or strategy was the most successful until now, there could be better options. Continually re-evaluate the merit and demerit of things.
- Do not get stuck in the past; the only thing that matters is performance. When investing, look at the current situation and see what is best. Do not linger onto those that have benefitted you before, but not as much anymore, nor to those who have harmed, but you have put in too much to pull out.

The Chapter Summary

CHAPTER 13

Developing a Professional Outlook (Corporate Image)

You cannot just do it; you have to look at the act too. However, creating professionalism is not just looks; it is a foundation for creating a good work environment to promote productivity and employee happiness. Nevertheless, professionalism isn't limited to the office but also the consumer side. Consumers should be dealt with professionally and feel like they are valued.

These days, it is just not enough to create a terrific product, offer super service, and have a solid business plan to back you up. Your company image is equally important to the overall success of your business.

Think about it. Every time you hand out your business card, send a letter or welcome a client into your office or store, you sell someone to your company. Your business card, letterhead, and signage—just like traditional print, radio, and TV ads—are valuable selling tools. The look of your office also helps *sell* your business by conveying an image, whether it is that of a funky, creative ad agency, or a staid, respectable accounting firm. Fortunately, just because you are a start-up company does not mean you have to look like one. Your logo, business card, signage, and style are part of a cohesive image program known as corporate identity. Furthermore, your company can appear highly professional with an authentic corporate identity and give the impression of having been in business for years.

In this chapter, we will discuss how to create a corporate image that works.

Everything in Its Place: The Office Space

When you are a startup with limited capital, it may be tempting to put all your money into advertising and equipment and skimp on office furniture. How you furnish your office might not seem to matter, especially if your customers will not see it. Moreover, if your office is located at home, the dining room table might look like the most logical choice.

Nevertheless, a nicely furnished office is not just a matter of aesthetics. Grabbing whatever furniture is at hand and plunking it down without a thought to an organization can put you at a significant disadvantage in terms of productivity.

Improving your own and your employees' performance involves a lot more than finding comfortable chairs. It involves the placement of offices or cubicles within the building, proximity to equipment, lighting, desk space, meeting areas, privacy, and more. People spend most of their waking hours at the office, so its design significantly affects morale.

How can you create a high-performance office? The first step is addressing organizational issues ... of who sits where. The days of big *power desks* and hierarchical corner offices are over. More businesses are turning to flexible environments ideal for small companies where the business owner probably doubles as salespeople.

With today's emphasis on team-building, office design moves away from compartmentalized offices and moves toward large spaces where teams of employees can work. When setting up your space, think about who needs to work with whom and which employees share what resources. If you group those people, you enhance their productivity. In addition to maximizing your own and your employees' productivity, your office may also function as a marketing tool if clients or customers visit.

The open office concept is fast emerging, initially promoted by silicon valley tech firms. The open office means everyone sits on the same floor; no one has a cabin or closed room. The cabins/closed rooms can be allocated for important meetings, primarily not to disturb others while speaking in a group. Facebook headquarters in Menlo Park, California, is an open plan to promote *friction-less working*. It is said to be the largest open office in the world.

Think about what visitors will see when they come by. Will they be bombarded with noise from one department near the entrance? Or will they see a series of closed doors with seemingly no activity taking place? Visitors should not be overwhelmed by chaos as they walk through your

Facebook HQ, Menlo Park California

building, but they should see signs of life and get glimpses of the daily activities going on at your company.

The primary factor for deciding your sitting space is the type of business dealing your firm does. Imagine you are a lawyers firm, where the client consultation is needed to be done in a private environment, then you may need to give individual rooms to the lawyers. Choose your arrangement after looking at your operational requirement.

Putting All in Place

Once considered some trendy European way to make business owners spend much money, ergonomics has gained respect. Simply put, this term refers to designing and arranging furnishings and space to fit the human body's natural movements. Ergonomics can help you and your employees avoid repetitive stress injuries from typing or bending and prevent joint problems, like back pain, which often sideline entrepreneurs and their employees.

Noise pollution is one of the biggest problems in many offices. One good way to decrease noise is to cover computer printers with sound shields. Covering a printer can cut noise by more than 90 percent; increase concentration accordingly.

Buy adjustable chairs. A good chair allows the user to adjust the seat height and the tension of the backrest. The seat should angle forward slightly to keep from cutting off your circulation. Boost the benefits of a good chair by providing footrests, and elevating the feet slightly while typing or sitting at a desk reduces lower back strain and improves circulation, keeping you more alert.

Make sure the desk and chair arrangement you choose allows you to keep the tops of your knuckles, the tops of your wrists, and your forearms all in a straight line as you work on your computer. Your computer monitor should be at or below your eye level. Use an under-desk keyboard tray and monitor stand, if necessary, to get everything in line.

Another often-ignored problem in offices is lighting. Too much or too little lighting causes eye strain and tiredness, decreasing productivity. To cut down on the glare, put filters on computer screens. Use individual lamps to illuminate desk work and help eyes adjust from overlit computer screens to underlit paper. Install miniblinds to let each employee control the amount of light to match the task at hand and the time of day.

You can find office furniture touted as ergonomic at various sources, from office supply superstores to traditional office furniture retailers. Just because something claims to be ergonomic, however, does not mean it is right for you. Always test furnishings before you buy them. Sit in the chair, make sure it is comfortable; sit at the desk, and make sure it is the right height. Make sure your desk and chair work together, and that there is plenty of legroom under the desk. When you buy furniture, look for solid construction, particularly on desks. The *ready to assemble* desks available at home or office superstores are often poor quality. Most are made of particleboard, which will not stand up to heavy use. A better option for those on a budget is to buy used office furniture.

More and more furniture dealers nowadays sell used (also called reconditioned) office furniture. You can find everything from a single desk and chair to an entire fleet of cubicles for your whole staff. Typically, furniture has been repaired and repainted where necessary. In some cases, you will be able to save 70 percent. You can find used furniture sources in the Yellow Pages or look in your local newspaper's classified ad section for individuals selling used pieces. Flea markets, auctions, and estate sales can be other sources of used items.

Logo Design

Before you start designing a business card or picking colors for your letterhead, you need a logo. Featuring your company name, embellished with a bit of color and perhaps a few graphic touches here and there, your logo is the essential design element because it is the basis for all your other materials: stationery, packaging, promotional materials, and signage.

Through the use of color and graphics, your logo should reflect the overall image you want your company to convey, advises Interbrand, a brand identity and marketing company. It should give people a feel for what your company is all about. Just by looking at a logo, a customer can identify your company from miles.

For example, say your product is an organic facial cream you will be marketing to health-conscious consumers. Your logo should represent your product's best benefits—being all-natural and environmentally sound. Creating a simple, no-nonsense logo using earth tones and a plain

Some of the best-known logos in the world

typeface will give the impression of a product that is *back to basics*, which is precisely what you want to achieve. Take that same product and give it a slick, high-tech look with neon colors; however, people will not associate your logo with the down-to-earth product you are selling. Logos come in two primary forms: abstract symbols (like the apple in Apple Computer) or logotypes, a stylized rendition of your company's name. You can also use a combination of both. Alan Siegel, chairman of Siegel+Gale, a design firm specializing in corporate identity, warns that promoting an abstract symbol can prove very costly for a small business on a budget. In addition, he says, such logos are harder to remember. "A logotype or wordmark is much easier to recall," says Siegel. "If you use an abstract symbol, always use it in connection with your business name."

Trying to create a logo on your own may seem like the best way to avoid the high costs of going to a professional design firm, which will charge thousands for a logo alone. However, be aware that many independent designers, including many who advertise online, charge much less. According to Stan Evenson, founder of Evenson Design Group, "Entrepreneurs on a tight budget should shop around for a designer. Many freelance designers charge rates ranging from $35 to $150 per hour, based on their experience. However, do not hire someone because of their bargain price. Find a designer who is familiar with your field ... and your competition. If the cost still seems exorbitant, remember that a good logo should last at least ten years. If you look at the amortization of that cost over ten years, it does not seem so bad."

Even if you have a good eye for color and a sense of what you want your logo to look like, you should still consult a professional designer. Why? They know whether or not a logo design will transfer quickly into print or onto a sign, while you might come up with a beautiful design that cannot be transferred or would cost too much to be printed. Your logo is the foundation for all your promotional materials, so this is one area where spending a little more now really pays off later.

Creating Your Business Cards

Once you have your logo, it is time to apply it to the marketing items you will use most, such as business cards. A sound business card should convey the overall image of your business—not easy, considering the card measures only 2 in. by 3 in. How can you possibly get a message across in such a small amount of space? You cannot expect your business card to tell the whole story about your company. What you should expect it to do is present a professional image people will remember. "A business card can make or break a client's first impression of your company," says Evenson. That little card makes as much of an impression as your appearance—the suit you wear or the briefcase you carry.

The color, wording, and texture of your business card have a lot to do with its appeal and its ability to convey your company image. Use commonsense when you are designing your business card. If your business markets children's toys and games, you might try using bright, primary colors and words written in a child's script. On the other hand, if you run a financial consulting service, you want your business card to convey professionalism and reliability, so stick to traditional looks such as black printing on a gray, beige, or white background.

Of course, professional designers claim entrepreneurs should not try to attempt designing a business card on their own, but many cash-strapped business owners have no other choice. The best course of action: Look at all the business cards you receive, and emulate the cards that you like. You have more leeway if you are in a creative business, such as party planning or retailing, but in general, keep the following tips in mind:

- Use your logo as the basis. Make it the most significant element on the card.
- Keep it simple. Do not cram too much information on the card.
- Include the essentials—your name, title, company name, address, phone and fax numbers, and e-mail and website addresses.
- Make sure the typeface is easily readable.
- Stick to one or two colors.
- Once you have got business cards, make the most of them.
- Always give people more than one card (so they can give it to others).
- Include your card in all correspondence.
- Carry cards with you at all times, in a card case, so they are clean and neat.

Stationery Selection

Every time you mail a letter to a prospective client or an existing customer, the missive leaves a long-lasting impression of your company. In a service business, your written materials are among your company's most essential marketing items. Moreover, if you run a home-based business that does not have a commercial location or sign, introducing your company to clients through the mail can be one of your most effective marketing techniques. The paper stock you choose and the colors and graphics embellishing it plays a vital role in your stationery's image. A neon pink stock may work well for a new suntan lotion manufacturer but not for an accounting service.

Your stationery should tie in with your business cards, featuring the same color scheme and overall look. Do not get so caught up in the design elements of your business stationery that you forget the obvious. Every piece of business stationery should include the basics: company name or logo, address, e-mail, and website addresses, and phone and fax numbers. You want to make it as easy as possible for your clients to respond to your offer by making all the information they need readily available. Attach your business card to each letter as well, so clients can put it in their Rolodexes for future reference.

Designing Your Sign

Retailers and restaurateurs alike realize the power of a good sign. Some companies rely on drive-by or walk-by traffic for customers, and if that is the case with your company, your sign may be the most crucial element of your entire corporate identity.

A promising sign must do more than just attract attention; it must also be readable from a reasonable distance. That is why, your original logo is so important—one that looks great on a small business card may not transfer well to a massive sign above your store. Going to a professional in the first stages of developing your image is essential. If you find out your great logo cannot be reproduced on a sign, you will have to go back to square one and rethink your logo, which will end up costing you more in the long run.

In recent years, a host of new signage materials has emerged to provide more variety and individuality. This also means it is harder to choose among all the possibilities, including neon, plastic, metal, wood, and more. Do some investigating before making your final decision; there is a wide range of prices for various materials. Depending on your location, sign placement can make a big difference, too. Options include a free-standing sign, a wall sign, a projecting sign, or a roof sign.

As you probably do not have the know-how or the equipment necessary to make a sign yourself, you will have to go to an outside manufacturer. Do not expect manufacturers to offer suggestions or point out any problems with your design if you have come up with one on your own. That is not their job. Before you head to the manufacturer with your design specifications, check your local zoning laws. You may find that the design you have come up with for your fried chicken restaurant—a 30-ft. neon number in the shape of a chicken—is not allowed in your area. If you are moving into a shopping center, the developer may have additional regulations governing signage that can be used in the facility.

Most entrepreneurs need professional assistance with signage because they do not have experience in this area. You probably will not know how big the letters should be visible from down the block, and you may not know which materials fare best in inclement weather. For this reason, you should visit a professional—either a designer or a sign fabricator.

A good designer knows when fabricators cut corners and not use the material requested or do a shoddy job. A designer will also be present at the installation time to make sure the sign is installed correctly.

The cost of a sign varies greatly depending on the materials, type of sign, and whether it has lighted. Buying directly from a fabricator can cost as little as 500 dollars, but you run the risk of not meeting zoning requirements. If you hire a designer, you will pay a design fee in addition to fabrication costs, but you have a better guarantee that the finished product will work for you.

Chapter Summary

- To be marketable, to be attractive to customers and investors, your business needs professionalism and a good appearance. A good corporate image goes a long way in making a good impression.
- No matter how large your office is, your interior and furniture should be very good. Investing in good chairs and tables and other office equipment will bolster productivity and make your employees' lives easier.
- Make systems and rules to keep the office organized, ensure each worker gets enough room, and have their essential work needs to be met.
- Put up some money for logo design; it is the first thing your customer sees with the name.
- A sound business card is excellent peer-to-peer marketing material. A solid business card may earn you customers, investors, or allies.

CHAPTER 14

Get Lucky—Taking Risky Decisions

Risk. Usually, people think of this wrongly, but actually, it is the only way to thrive. Do not see risk in terms of loss; see it in terms of probability and the losses associated with those probabilities. If you have a 50 percent of losing two million dollars of a business valued at 10 million, do not go for it. Why? The odds are not in your favor, and there is too much at stake.

Risk is a choice.

Popular books about entrepreneurship frequently imply that entrepreneurs get lucky by taking huge risks. This is a myth! Most successful entrepreneurs are actually very cautious. They take risks, certainly, but they get lucky by de-risking their ventures as much as possible.

This chapter explains how to approach risky decisions. We begin by reminding ourselves what risk is (and is not) and what attracts us to the wrong kind of risk. We then consider strategies for handling risky opportunities.

What Is Risk?

Intuitively, we tend to see risk as the possibility or the probability of something bad happening to us like being burgled, the factory catching fire or suddenly going bankrupt. In this view, things go wrong, and there is not much that we can do about it. Yet the word *risk* actually derives from the early Italian word risicare, which means *to dare*. This definition implies four things:

1. Risk is not a fate but a choice.
2. We choose whether or not to take a risk.
3. We bring most of our misfortunes on ourselves.
4. Risk is something that can, to an extent, be managed and controlled.

Why Bad Risks Attract

Being lucky means doing better than an objective analysis of the situation would suggest. A bad risk is a risk that is much bigger than an objective analysis of the situation would reasonably justify.

Imagine an unhappy day at the races. You have lost 95 dollars in failed bets and have just five dollars left. Do you bet your last five dollars on the favorite running at odds of say 3 to 1 or on a long shot running at odds of 20 to 1? Logically it makes sense to bet on the favorite as there is a small possibility of emerging with 15 dollars, either that or not bet at all. You may well prefer, however, to risk it all on the long shot even though you will probably only end up with nothing. The decidedly riskier choice attracts because your attention is riveted on the 95 dollars you have lost, and the longshot bet offers an opportunity to recoup that loss. Recall, however, that the 95 dollars is irrelevant because it cannot influence future outcomes. Remove that reference point from the equation and you will see the decision for what it is; that is, a choice of how best to invest five dollars.

We tend to become risk-seeking when we see ourselves as faced with a choice between losses. To be more precise, the prospect theory predicts that faced with a choice between: (1) accepting a sure loss at time and (2) the possibility of avoiding that loss altogether but at the risk of subsequently incurring a much bigger loss at time, we may be tempted to avoid a sure loss even though we may be risking catastrophe.

Although the prospect theory was developed for clear-cut choices involving precise mathematical probabilities, it may well be relevant to many business decisions where the issues are rather more amorphous. Risk-seeking behavior may explain, for example, why accountant Arthur Andersen ended up being dragged down with Enron, the collapsed energy firm. All that probably happened initially was that Andersen stretched the rules a little. The following year they stretched them a little further, and so on. Taking the ethical path by subsequently refusing the client's demands and/or reporting their misdemeanors would have invited punishment. There is also the possibility that firms like Andersen become caught in the so-called consistency trap. That is, our perceived need as human beings to display consistency demands that having agreed to something in Year 1, we will agree to it subsequently. Likewise, a hotelier may be tempted to serve food that has passed its use-by date. More specifically, the temptation is to avoid a relatively small loss by discarding the food. The risk is that the hotelier subsequently incurs a much bigger loss, financial and reputational, if guests suffer food poisoning.

Notice, however, that there is a choice to be made. Disaster is by no means inevitable. The ethical path stands open. There is no law that requires us to be consistent. Nor is there any ambiguity about whether the hotelier should use the food. If disaster happens, it happens through choice. Remember: you make your decisions and your decisions make you.

On the Rebound

We are most likely to become risk-seeking when things are going badly. In the early 1990s, sales of Coca-Cola were declining. "You can extrapolate that out and end up with zilch," said Robert Goizueta, Coke's President and Chief Operating Officer. Coca-Cola decided that drastic circumstances called for drastic action, and so, they tried to reverse their fortunes by changing the formula. The resultant public outcry forced the company to reverse the decision after only three months.

Steiff, makers of luxury teddy bears, made a similar mistake when they decided to compete on price instead of quality and accordingly switched production to China. Steiff thought they had done their homework properly. Indeed, they were prepared for the obvious risks such as safety and poor-quality stitching. It was the more subtle snags that defeated the plan. Steiff did not realize that it would take eight months to a year to train new seamstresses (more used to making microchips) to an adequate standard. Transport costs also proved higher than expected. Ships were frequently overbooked or Steiff would pay premium prices to book space in advance only to find that the bears were not ready to ship. After five years, Steiff abandoned the strategy and moved production back to Europe.

Disappointment can also trigger rash behavior. Just as the jilted lover frequently seeks a new (and often unsuitable) partner on the rebound, entrepreneurs may react to disappointment by making a very risky move to compensate.

Sarah expanded her hairdressing business from a *one woman* plus occasional assistant, to a large emporium with five chairs to rent to other hairdressers. Sarah discovered, however, that she was actually worse off as a result, as additional revenues were simply consumed by higher rents and other expenses. Disappointed, she immediately decided to open another salon, renting out more chairs to more stylists. A week before she was due to sign the contract for her second shop, Sarah changed her mind. She decided the move was too risky.

She said, "I worked it out if I open several shops and make a little bit of profit from each one it could work out quite good but the big risk is the second shop. When you get to the third shop you've already got two shops full of staff and the chance of them both going under is unlikely but when you do your first of two shops, if the staff walked out from this shop for instance I'd have to find $500 a week rent."

Sarah decided to wait a few months and then look for safer opportunities to expand. Not everyone pulls back in time. It was a wise decision because, as Sarah recognized, it is the second venture rather than the first that can be the big opportunity and the big risk. If it goes wrong, it can destroy both businesses, but if it goes well, it can provide the launch pad platform for exponential expansion. So, it pays to be patient and get it right.

Managing Big Risks

The British Isles have not been invaded often because of the risks involved. The last successful attempt was in 1066 when Duke William of Normandy set forth without so much as a basic *SatNav* to guide him on his way. This daring enterprise succeeded because the astute duke was very careful to de-risk it. First, he persuaded Tostig to land a diversionary force in the north of England ahead of the main invasion. Second, after the Battle of Hastings, William kept his ships within hail as he progressed through southern England.

"Be bold but cautious."

Like Duke William, many successful entrepreneurs are bold in their ideas but cautious in executing them. Business analysts predicted that

Richard Branson's decision to enter the aviation industry was doomed to fail. Branson, however, was careful to de-risk the bold decision by leasing rather than buying planes so that if it went wrong, his exposure would be limited. Things might have gone better for Coke if they had done some small-scale market testing of their new brand rather than taken a *big bang* approach.

De-risking can take many forms. *Just-in-time* delivery arrangements can reduce the risk of incurring a cash flow crisis by minimizing the cost of holding stock. Buying a franchise can reduce start-up risks. Forming a consortium can spread risk among several parties. Another possibility is to use a counterbalance by combining high- and low-risk elements. For instance, opera houses staging works by obscure composers counterbalance the risk of empty seats by engaging well-known composers likely to attract the crowds.

The Patel Strategy

Of course, you cannot de-risk everything. Ultimately, there is nothing for it but for entrepreneurs to "play their cards and take their chances." One of the most famous risks taken in business history was Tom Spencer's decision to invest his life savings in Michael Marks's small retail empire. Marks had already come a long way in a short time from his days as an itinerant pedlar selling buttons, thread, and other small items from a small tray when he met Spencer. Moreover, Spencer must have been impressed by Marks's success and his energy and ambition. Even so, it was a big risk. There was no welfare state in those days, so Spencer would have been destitute in old age if it had gone wrong. As we now know, the risk paid off handsomely. While Marks worked hard running the business and opening new stores, Spencer retired to the country and rapidly drank himself to death on the proceeds of a business that still bears his name even though he never actually worked for it.

> *"High risk: high reward = good*
> *Low risk: high reward = better."*

Although high risks can be justified by high reward, there is another, possibly better, way to get rich known as the Patel approach. The Patels had very little money, so they concentrated upon buying cheap motels where the profits were good, the risks of failure low, and the financial consequences containable. Eventually, the Patels built a chain of motels all over the United States, and as a result, they became extremely wealthy. It is the difference between the *hare* and the *tortoise*.

Keep Your Options Open

Why do we fit locks on doors? Unless you are an economist or a police officer, you have probably never given the question a moment's thought! Intuitively you might say, "to stop people from breaking in." Yet, locks are only fitted if the trouble and expense are justified. After the suicide bomb attacks on the London Underground in July 2005, an alert police officer checking a property noticed that a new and expensive padlock had been fitted to an old garden shed. Why go to all that trouble, reasoned the officer; what did the shed contain that was worth protecting? The officer's curiosity was rewarded with the discovery of a stash of explosives.

Like fitting locks on doors, the options theory assumes that there is economic value in resolving uncertainty and capturing opportunities. An option creates the right but not the obligation to take an action in the future. For example, if you manufacture orange juice, you may want to know what you are going to have to pay for oranges in a year's time. It is a tricky question because so much can change meanwhile. Rather than try to guess the price and risk getting it wrong, you could purchase an option that gives you the right to buy say 10,000 tons of oranges in a year's time at 10c each. If in a year's time, oranges cost 9c, the option expires, worthless. If the price of oranges has risen to 11c, however, the option is exercised, and the party granting it stands the loss. Whatever happens, you can be sure that you will pay no more than 10c for your oranges.

Options are most commonly used where a business revolves around currency exchanges or involves dealing in commodities, but they can be deployed in a variety of contexts. For example, Hewlett Packard chose a portfolio approach in designing printers. That is, rather than guess which type of input slot was likely to prove most popular and risk getting it wrong, HP decided to incorporate all four industry standards into the design. The purchase price of the option in this case is in higher production costs. The pay-off is increased consumer appeal. Likewise, an entrepreneur might purchase an option to buy out a partner, or to abandon research and development (R&D) ventures, or, like Branson and his planes, use leases to defer full investment.

Options are also a way of exploiting opportunities. There is seldom opportunity without some kind of risk, but, by definition, opportunity is the flip side of risk. For instance, many initial risky investments, such as opening up operations abroad, create follow-on possibilities for further expansion. Expansion is not compulsory, but should local conditions favor it, the entrepreneur can increase manufacturing capacity or diversify the range of products made. Whereas a firm that concentrates its operations in a single location must cope with all the turbulence and uncertainty that arises there, a firm that is spread geographically can transfer activities from one location to another.

There are five different types of options:

1. Immediate entry
2. Immediate exit
3. Delayed entry
4. Delayed exit
5. Shadow option

Let us consider each in turn.

Immediate Entry

An immediate entry option involves advancing a small amount in order to create or acquire the right to purchase a full commitment later. For example, placing a deposit on a car buys you the right but not the obligation to purchase the vehicle in the future. You simply lose your deposit if you decide not to proceed (though an entrepreneur would probably sell his or her place in the queue at a handsome profit!).

Immediate entry options are particularly valuable where a decision is time-critical or dependent upon exclusive rights. Apple clinched a two-year lead over competitors by securing the rights to miniature hard drives central to the iPod music player design. Employing people on work experience programs is another form of immediate entry option. Such programs enable you to test prospective employees before deciding whether to employ them. (Incidentally, another benefit is that potential employees are more likely to return to a firm if they have worked there before.) A firm with a fledgling factory abroad might acquire options to buy land, should they subsequently wish to expand.

Immediate Exit

An immediate exit option involves making a full commitment but acquires the right to reverse it immediately. For example, rather than take the risk of employing engineers, a software development company may hire them on a consultancy basis. While this is a more expensive solution than employing people, if a contract is canceled or work dries up for some other reason, the company can immediately rid itself of surplus staff. Likewise, some landlords rent office space and industrial units on an immediate exit basis. The rents are higher than traditional leases, but the corollary is that the tenant may only be required to give a week's notice.

Delayed Entry

Delayed entry options are useful where entering and exiting the market involves an expensive *all or nothing* commitment. Oil exploration companies, for example, may decide to acquire the land and the necessary licences but postpone drilling until they have conducted detailed geological investigations. The advantage of paying for such an option is that subsequent decisions about whether or not to drill are based upon much better information than would otherwise be possible. Likewise, a speculative builder might acquire land banks cheaply in the midst of a recession but delay construction unless and until property prices reached a certain level.

Delayed Exit

Whereas a delayed entry option allows you to buy time before making an expensive investment, a delayed exit option allows you to buy time before abandoning a project. Delayed exit options are useful where exiting from a venture is so expensive that the decision is virtually irreversible. For example, if the price of say gold or diamonds falls to such a level that mining no longer makes economic sense, rather than close down the mine completely and sell off the land, it might be wise to mothball its pending developments. It costs money to keep the mine in commission, but it is much cheaper than opening a completely new one. Delayed exit options proved popular during the so-called credit crunch of 2009 as many construction companies decided to mothball plans to build flats and houses.

Shadow Options

Shadow options emerge unexpectedly. A vet assisting in a branch surgery learns about how to run a business as well as gaining clinical knowledge and experience. Suddenly the principal decides to sell. The assistant's experience makes the option of buying the business much less risky than it would otherwise have been.

Shadow options can work the other way, too. Sam owned an antiques business for many years. As fashions changed, the business gradually became non-viable, and Sam eventually sold the building he owned. He was then invited to manage an antiques business for someone he had known as a competitor for many years. "It's great," said Sam. "I shut the door and go home. I don't have to worry about anything."

Sam's career as an owner created this shadow option. Firms that share knowledge and experience informally can create a *shadow option* by paving the way for joint ventures. Such firms may have a flying start compared to firms that plunge into the unknown.

Even failure can create a shadow option. For instance, shelved R&D projects can re-emerge. Attempts in the early 1980s to create small handheld computers capable of reading handwritten text were complete failures. Yet, these prototypes eventually became the commercially successful Palm Pilots of the new millennium.

Although shadow options emerge unexpectedly, entrepreneurs can get lucky by purchasing a few. Entrepreneurs can increase the number of *cards* in their hands by investing here and there, diversifying a little, becoming involved in some committees, and so forth. After all, what are time and money for, if not for risking? Many if not most potential shadow options will fizzle away. The point is that almost certainly one or two will come into the money.

Caveat Emptor

Options encourage entrepreneurs to address fundamental sources of uncertainty rather than merely hoping everything will turn out for the best. That said, options cannot solve all problems of risk and uncertainty. Moreover, they come at a price and, since they are difficult to value, they may not always be worth what you paid for them. Consultants may insist upon a guarantee of a fixed number of days' work a year, thus obviating part of the value of an immediate exit option. The risk, moreover, may not always be confined to the initial purchase price of the option. For instance, in practice, switching production from one country to another can be a complex and problematic exercise. Keeping an option open like a mine or an oil platform may require ongoing investment. Delayed exit options may provide an excuse for escalation. Pursuing shadow options can deflect energy and resources into sideshows that detract from the pursuing of a coherent strategy. Indeed, purchasing lots of small options may be more costly than living with the uncertainty. Ultimately, it is a case of caveat emptor (let the buyer beware).

Even so, used carefully, options are a potential weapon in the entrepreneur's armory against risk. The best way to manage options is to be specific. Investigate carrying costs, be clear about what needs to happen before an option is exercised, and ensure that the capability exists to support the option meanwhile. For example, specify in advance at what price a partner will be bought out. The alternative is to be left haggling later.

The value of options increases with uncertainty. Shadow options are perhaps the most interesting of all because they can occur by chance as well as design. Indeed, you could perhaps say that all of life experience is a potential *shadow option* that might one day be exercised.

Chapter Summary

- Risks must be taken for any reward.
- Bad risks attract, do not try to recoup from a loss by investing in the same thing further. The odds are against you.
- You are more likely to take risks when things go south, do not.
- High risk and high reward is good, low risks and high reward is even better. Look for the most reward value out of any risk you choose to take.
- Keep your options open, never all in until you are confident, or if the next step will win you big.
- Always look for shadow options.

CHAPTER 15

Be What You Can Be— Decisionless Decisions and the Psychology of Success

As we have stated before, taking risks is essential for healthy growth. If you do not take the risk, you will be crushed by the competition. Be an intelligent gambler; only play when the odds are in your favor and only terrible risk decisions with little to no investment. It is simple: more money to what is in your favor and less to what is not. Taking too little risk can be worse than taking too much.

It is afternoon at the market. Fruit vendors are calling, "Pick your own bananas! One dollar a kg! Come on now, ladies! Pick your bananas!" Another stall-holder shouts, "Margarine! Plenty of margarine!"

It starts raining. A trader grapples with plastic sheeting to protect his stock. His neighbor advises him not to bother. "You can't damage damaged goods!" he jokes.

Beneath the banter lurks anxiety. Before, being a market trader was a sure route to prosperity, particularly for a trader in the indoor market. Times have changed, however. January and February were known as *kipper months* because of the quiet post-Christmas trading. Now almost every month is a *kipper*. Gone are the days when flower-sellers carried their takings home in buckets and spent all of Sunday counting out the copper and silver coins and when grocers could pile their counters high with pork pies and expect to be sold out by 5 o'clock. "Stalls [in the indoor market] were like gold dust," said a trader. "You couldn't get one for love nor money."

Now, hardly a week passes without another trader pulling down the shutters for good. "This stall is in a good position," said a trader, "but what can you do when people aren't even stopping to look?"

What indeed? Significantly, it is often the most prosperous traders who have suffered worst. We will explore later why that is the case. Here it is sufficient to note that whereas the previous chapter concerned excessive risk taking, this chapter considers:

- Why too little risk can be even more dangerous than too much
- What makes us afraid of risk
- How to overcome fear of risk

The Psychology of Success

Which would you prefer:

- A sure gain of 500,000 dollars
- A 50 per cent chance to win one million dollars or, alternatively, nothing at all?

Most of us would probably opt for a sure gain of 500,000 dollars because although it is a lot less than one million dollars, it would enable us to do important things like paying off a mortgage, providing for school fees, or providing a comfortable cushion in retirement.

Supposing, however, the choice were between:

- A sure gain of 10,000 dollars
- A 50 percent chance to win one million dollars?

Unless we are absolutely desperate for 10,000 dollars, the optimal choice is to gamble on winning one million dollars. Although it is risky, because you could end up with nothing, the risk is justified by the potential reward.

Yet it is a risk that not everyone would take. The prospect theory predicts that gains that are certain tend to be preferable to those that are merely probable, even though the latter may be much more valuable than the former.

"If you are consistently successful, is it because you are not taking enough risk?"

The prospect theory may explain why some entrepreneurs stop short of achieving their full potential and why some highly prosperous businesses eventually melt down. In a nutshell, the theory implies that entrepreneurs may hesitate to take risks for fear of jeopardizing what they already have. Indeed, this is what stops many people from becoming entrepreneurs in the first place: fear of giving up a nice, steady job.

Peter owned four stalls in an indoor market. He made a very good living. The chance arose to acquire a stall in a market 20 miles away. This was in the days when stalls were like gold dust, and Peter decided to proceed. The experiment lasted barely a fortnight. "This is doing my head in," said Peter's assistant. "It's doing my head in too," replied Peter, so they walked away. In retrospect, Peter believes that the decision to quit was a mistake. "I see now that I could have branched out from there but at the time I was afraid that it would pull me away from my main line of business."

"You can't make an omelette without breaking eggs."

Peter's fear of becoming distracted is tantamount to a fear of endangering existing gains. Such reluctance can affect big, sophisticated firms too. For example, Goldman Sachs enjoyed a huge run of prosperity during the 1980s. In the early 1990s, many partners were reluctant to experiment with new ventures such as government bonds. Why upset the golden goose?

Goldman Sachs was highly successful and the partnership was by its nature conservative. After a decade of astounding prosperity, the impetus for change was low. "We were moving too slowly or not at all, to face some serious competitive threats ... If we waited to fix them it might get too late."

The firm was only propelled into those new markets, thanks to the determination of two far-sighted partners, Stephen Friedman and Robert Rubin, who recognized that current levels of prosperity were unsustainable. "If you are not constantly working for constructive strategic change, then you are steward of something that must erode," said Stephen Friedman.

On a Roll

The proverb states that a bird in hand is worth two in the bush. In business, however, as Friedman and Rubin recognized, the apparently safer option may not be safe for very long. No law guarantees that an existing line of business will be viable for ever, however prosperous it may be and however rock-solid certain that prosperity may seem. Sam made a fortune from opening up shops on short leases, closing them down again when the lease expired, and opening up somewhere else. Sam describes the business in its heyday:

"You'd get there with the staff about quarter past six in the morning and by half past seven people were in the shop and they were buying ... I'd say possibly that queue would be 35 people long—all the way round that counter out into the street ... till half past four—it was non-stop ... you were literally run off your feet ... The wholesalers ... once or twice they'd open up for us on a Saturday ... because you just couldn't get enough ... [stock] in the shop ... I couldn't have done better if I'd won the [football] pools. "

The first ominous note was sounded by Sam's accountant. He asked Sam where he thought the business would be in 10 years' time. Sam said:

"I was flying high at that point. I said, 'What do you mean?' He said, 'Where do you think you'll be in ten years' time?' I said, 'Well, I hope I'll still be in business and making a living.' But you do, you think it's never going to end."

However, it did end. Within less than 10 years, as supermarkets put many small shops out of business, Sam ended up with only one outlet and only a fraction of his former wealth.

"Doing nothing is a risky decision."

Recall, risk is a choice. Sam could see no reason to change his business model as he was making a fortune. Yet doing nothing, *business as usual*, is itself a risky choice. It is what we academics call a *decisionless decision*. Decisionless decisions have consequences, just like any other decision. Outcomes—for better, for worse; for richer, for poorer—are determined by inaction as well as action.

Entrapment

The trouble is, the impact of *decisionless decisions* becomes apparent only when it is too late to reverse them. Continuity begets continuity. Entrepreneurs can become trapped in a sub-optimal venture through the simple passage of time. Entrapment happens because time is an investment and one that is every bit as important as money—possibly more important in the long run.

In the 1950s, Val's hairdressing salon was the epitome of elegance and luxury: white net curtains, white wood furniture offering a temporary escape from the omnipresent dirt and damp of a sooty town and houses with cold taps, stone sinks, and outside toilets. It was a thriving business with both sinks and all four driers in regular commission.

Forty years later, the business was still going but generating barely enough money to keep Val in a modest standard of living. It was not hard to see why. The upholstery of two chairs was split. One sink looked as if it had not been used for years—a picture of rust, cobwebs, and grime. The towels looked tired. The white plastic *curlers* were covered in a gray, greasy film of dirt. The walls and surfaces were damp and had patches of black mold. The electrics were the original 1950s, yellowing and probably dangerous. The net curtains had been transformed from white to black. The years had taken their toll on the client list too, as death and population movements had reduced the numbers little by little.

"How does a business decline? One day at a time."

The decline was partly due to Val's decision not to employ staff. Recall, employing people is an important route to prosperity because you can extract a surplus from their labor. Val was risk-averse. She did not want the bother of possibly having to get rid of staff, so she took the apparently safer option. Compounding the decline was Val's tendency to hide behind the net curtains, ignoring new hairstyles and treatments, instead carrying on with the familiar perms and *shampoo and set* that she felt safe with.

As Val's story shows, there is a price to be paid for remaining within one's comfort zone—whether it is technology we understand or business practices that have worked well in the past. Furthermore, once a business begins to decline, the process becomes progressively harder to reverse because a vicious circle is set in motion. As the business declines, funds for reinvestment become scarcer. It, therefore, becomes harder to retain customers and attract new ones. Consequently, the decline deepens. Eventually the business becomes a shadow of its former self, living on borrowed time.

Some big firms also hide behind metaphorical net curtains. Marks & Spencer clung to their tried-and-tested formula long after high street retail practices had moved on. It took the imminent threat of meltdown to persuade management to offer customers facilities such as changing rooms and the acceptance of external credit cards. More recently, Woolworths paid the ultimate price for seemingly being trapped in a terminal time warp.

Thriving on Fear

Fear holds us back more than anything else. To calculate the opportunity cost imparted by fear, list all the things you would do if you were not afraid.

"What would you do if you were not afraid?"

The first step in shrinking fear is to identify what you are afraid of. Be specific: fear feeds on vague terrors.

"What exactly are you afraid of?"

Having isolated the problem, then deal with it. There are two schools of thought. One is to "feel the fear and do it anyway"; the other is to wait until you feel reasonably comfortable about making a move and then make it. Both approaches have something to recommend them. The advantage of the former is that by doing, you will probably make the fear vanish. The risk is that if you are really afraid, you may not do it very well and end up failing as a result of fear. The advantage of acting with a fair degree of confidence is that you are more likely to succeed. The disadvantage is endless procrastination. If possible, combine both approaches. Again, the 80/20 rule is a good one. That is, wait until your very worst fears have subsided, feel the residual 20 percent fear and then do it anyway. You should analyze the market before launching a new product. The danger is that you can analyze the market for ever. So, do some analysis and then try to achieve your first sale.

DIY Risk Assessment

Another technique for confronting fear is to conduct a risk assessment. Risk assessment works by listing all the main risks that you can think of surrounding a venture and then multiplying the probability and impact to arrive at a risk score.

Imagine you are considering acquiring a company. Your worst fear may be that the acquisition becomes a cultural misfit with your existing operations—a risk that is quite high because of the differences between the two operations. So, you score the likelihood of that risk becoming a reality as 7 out of 10. Next, consider the possible impact of the risk. It could be quite significant as most mergers between large firms founder on cultural tensions that destroy rather than create value. So, you score it as 8 out of 10. Now multiply 7 by 8, making a total risk score of 56 out of 100. When you think about mitigations, however, you realize that you could organize the takeover in such as way that everyone, including staff in your own firm, has to apply for their own job. That would create an opportunity to exclude cultural misfits and remove poor performers from your own firm. On the other hand, you have to ask yourself whether the cure would be worse than the disease. That is, would the resultant tension and uncertainty precipitate a meltdown of both firms, a very serious risk if a *people* business is involved? On the other hand, can you afford to let this opportunity pass you by? If you don't do this now, where might you be in 10 years' time?

Risk assessment is a useful weapon in decision making, but it is by no means foolproof. Risk has a sense of humor. You may think you have covered all the major risks and then the unexpected happens. Moreover, risk assessment is an inherently subjective exercise because there is little objective guidance on how to assign numbers to probabilities and impacts. Even so, working through the process does at least reduce risk and quantify vague terrors.

Speculating to Accumulate

Being wrong about something can be a very good thing. If you play the lottery, you are almost certain to get it wrong, but that does not mean that the decision to invest a dollar is a disaster. Far from it! Where the stakes are small and the pay-off is sufficiently large, we should carry on investing even though we accumulate failure after failure. Fear of being wrong often prevents us from seeing opportunity—the flip side of risk. Fear of being wrong is deeply ingrained in us from school onwards. The *ticks and crosses* approach to learning instills fear and ignores shades of gray. When Marks & Spencer opened their store on London's Oxford Street in the 1930s, it was by no means certain that the venture would be profitable. The decision went ahead, though, because the company reckoned that even if the store made a loss, having a presence in such a prestigious location would benefit the chain as a whole.

Risk Assessment Checklist

List all the main risks involved in a venture.

1. How probable is this risk on a score of 1 to 10?
2. What would the impact be on a score of 1 to 10?
3. Multiply the two results to achieve a risk score.
4. What could I do to reduce the probability?
5. What could I do to minimize the impact?
6. What might be the cost of not taking the risk?

Adapt and Survive

Town and city markets may have declined, but there is still money to be made. The most promising survivors are typically those who have moved with the times, making small but significant, low-risk changes to the business such as replacing old, greasy, handwritten signs with brightly colored laminates, investing in a new display, experimenting with new lines, listening to customers, and picking up ideas for adding value from trade magazines and trying them out.

The attraction of this strategy is that it avoids the much bigger risk involved in completely revamping the business. Some ideas work, others don't. The point is, any losses are small, and therefore, the damage is limited. Moreover, a series of small changes can add up to more than the sum of their parts.

Always provided that you are willing to *give it a go*, that is. Michael was a successful fishmonger who owned a large house and a Bentley. Michael had been selling fish all his life. The shop was taking over 50,000 dollars a week. He recalls how his daughter started badgering him to start selling new lines like bass and sea bream in addition to the traditional cod, haddock, plaice, and kippers. Michael refused to hear of it. He then went on holiday, leaving his daughter to run the business: "I remember going on holiday and I left her in charge. All the time she's has been saying we ought to get all these [new] fish." 'Oh! No! No! No!—too dear.'

I came back and I remember the bill was about 25 percent more than it had been [in] the previous weeks before we'd gone on holiday. I looked at it and she'd bought all these things. I didn't know what she'd taken at that point, but I thought, 'Oh crikey! It's going to be a disaster is this.'

Notice what happens here. The business is taking 50,000 dollars a week, and Michael is worried about a few extra boxes of fish. The point is, even if the experiment failed, the risk was justified, given the level of turnover. Michael, however, is more afraid of risking existing gains than excited by future possibilities. Besides, the experiment succeeded. Michael again: And it hadn't been [a disaster]. Then you realized, people wanted other things; they wanted bass and they wanted squids and they wanted prawns. I would say now that probably without [new lines] we wouldn't be able to urvive at the rents and rates that we pay and the cost of staff.

Moral: do it.

The market traders we most wanted to interview were the ones who were no longer there, that is, those who sold up when stalls were still like gold dust. How did they recognize that the metaphorical clock was turning half-past 11? We will probably never know the answer. One possibility is that they looked at return on capital employed as well as the more usual yardsticks of profit and turnover. If you have say 100,000 dollars invested in an enterprise and the annual profit is 5,000 dollars (5 percent), you would actually be better putting the money in the bank if it would earn 6.5 percent there. Lowering of return on capital employed can be an early warning sign that midnight is approaching.

The Dangers of Herding

A word of caution: don't do something just because everyone else is doing it. Why do Harry Potter books sell millions? The reason may well be because millions have already been sold. Economists call it herding.

Imagine a row of restaurants. They are all empty except one, which contains two diners. You might decide that the latter probably has something to commend it as two people have chosen to eat there. So you follow suit, and so do the next couple and the next. In each case, the decision to eat there is made on an assumption rather than hard information about the quality of the food.

Resist the temptation to follow the herd. Members of a herd are not making informed decisions and could therefore be heading over a cliff—like the banks caught up in the sub-prime mortgage market. As the market for conventional mortgages became saturated, banks looked for alternatives. They started lending to people whose credit ratings would not otherwise qualify them for a loan. Other banks followed suit—ignoring the precept that the art of banking is to lend money to customers who can afford to repay the loan, not to charge higher rates of interest to people likely to default after two or three years. Beware also computer herding. One of the reasons why banks all end up ensnared in the same mess is that they all use the same software programs to analyze risks and make investment decisions.

Fortunes have been made by moving in the opposite direction to the herd—selling when others are buying, investing when others are holding off, and so on. During the run-up to deregulation (the Big Bang) in 1986, most of London's traditional broking and jobbing firms scrambled to find buyers among the giant U.S. investment banks—with Cazenove as a notable exception. The firm's partners stood largely aloof from it all, reasoning that there would be a market for truly independent advice in the post-Big Bang era. The influential *Financial Times* newspaper disagreed with this assessment and predicted that Cazenove's independence would prove short-lived. In fact, Cazenove survived and prospered for 15 years before finally merging with J P Morgan.

Quantum Shifts

Adaptation has limits. The stagecoach companies and canal boat owners of old responded to the threat posed by competition from railways by instituting express services that raised their *game* from around 6 km an hour to around 16. The strategy was successful for a while because rail travel was initially slow and unreliable, but ultimately, the earlier forms of transport were doomed.

"Stick to the knitting, but not for ever."

Nothing is immune from time's erosion. We will always need teachers, but many university education departments in the UK became virtually redundant when the government changed the method of training. We will always need dentists, but improved standards of living and better health education mean that we need far fewer. There will always be criminals, but lawyers who specialized in criminal law, expecting a comfortable living, have found their livelihoods undermined by reductions in legal aid payments.

Profound change cannot be halted, but the effects can usually be anticipated by engaging in simple scenario planning. What would you do if X, Y, or Z happened?

"It pays to think the unthinkable occasionally."

Go Higher

The unthinkable does happen. Sam's business was prosperous, but its prosperity was built upon sand. The most enduring entrepreneurs create a legacy. This means more than owning a string of businesses and dabbling in all manner of investments from slot machines to recycling paper clips.

Be what you can be, promises the U.S. army recruiting slogan. Why not create something unique like Anita Roddick's Body Shop, Tim Farmer's Kwik Fit, or James Dyson's vacuum cleaners? It may be no more work and no more risky or difficult than mere ownership. It will not render you immune from competition, copying of ideas, and time's erosion, but there is the pivotal advantage of being first in the field, to say nothing of the satisfaction of inscribing your signature.

Developing a Healthy Definition of Success

Still afraid of taking a risk and stepping out into the unknown? You are not alone. It is not uncommon for even experienced entrepreneurs to measure themselves against unreasonable standards and see themselves falling short. For example, a successful entrepreneur in the UK once admitted that he thought his business was a failure. This was unusual because there was no doubt in my mind (or anyone else's) that he was doing quite well.

"How long have you been in business?" He was asked.

"Sixteen years," he replied.

"And how many similar businesses around here have come and gone during that time?"

"Seven," he answered.

"What about your salary? Do you make a good living?"

"Oh yes," he replied. "I have got a nice car, I live in one of the better parts of town, and I usually take two vacations a year."

"Tell me about your employees. Do they leave every few months, or do they stay with you?"

"All of them have been with me for years."

"I am sorry," I said, "maybe I am missing something. Where do you think you are going wrong?"

He got the point. He was confusing his desire to do better with failure. Like so many people, he saw other entrepreneurs who had more of something than he did, and he immediately assumed that he was losing. The message? Be reasonable with your expectations and learn to view your business goals as a staircase rather than a one-chance shot to the moon. This does not mean settling for less; it means being realistic and progressive when it comes to your aspirations. As one entrepreneur I interviewed put it, "Tell your readers that the fear and insecurity of running a business never ends. Indeed, the very concept of entrepreneurship involves overcoming the daily nagging dread that even after serving a satisfied customer, we are, in effect, unemployed until the next customer can be secured. It is just something we entrepreneurs have to learn to live with."

Chapter Summary

- Taking too little risk can lead to more harm than taking too much.
- Taking risks is essential to growth, and when the norm is taking risks, playing it safe becomes a disadvantage.
- Inaction has consequences, and inaction has its risks.
- Fear is terrible, but just enough leads to cautionary risk-taking, which is our ideal.
- Risk assessments are a useful way to evaluate risks.
- Adapting to market changes puts you ahead of those who do not. It is not a winning strategy; it is a survival one.
- Do not do things just because everyone else is doing it.
- Change cannot be halted, but preparing and anticipating always helps.

Summary

1. Developing the Vision and Business Idea

To have a great idea, have a lot of them. And there is far more opportunity than there is ability. Developing a business idea is usually the first challenge faced by every entrepreneur when starting a business from scratch. Finding the right business opportunity or creatively developing an idea is certainly not an easy task. Envisioning the idea the first true task of an entrepreneur. An entrepreneur must possess the ability to see what others cannot see. While others see problems, an entrepreneur must see opportunities. But seeing opportunities is just the beginning. The main business challenge is going to be the ability to forge that opportunity into a business idea. This is a business challenge because the process of transforming problems into business opportunities is like trying to turn lead into gold. The entrepreneurial process of creating value out of nothing; a process that brings innovative products into existence. The following is an illustration of how the process goes:

Identifying a problem > Seeing an opportunity in the problem > Coming up with a solution > Forging the opportunity into a business idea > Integrating the solution into a business plan.

Developing a vision is definitely a business challenge because an entrepreneur must sometimes assume the role of a sorcerer. Most individuals are comfortable with the present way of doing things, but it is the duty of an entrepreneur to envision and forecast the future. An entrepreneur must always be ahead of his time or else he will lose his relevance. It is the duty of an entrepreneur to bring into present what is yet to be. It is also the duty of an entrepreneur to bring solutions to other people's problems. In the late 1970s and early 1980s, while IBM saw increase in demand for their mainframe computers, Steve Jobs envisioned a personal computer in every home and Bill Gates envisioned the need for easy-to-use software for personal computers. That single vision made Bill Gates the richest man in the world and Steve Jobs the most famous business person of the 21st century. A good businessman must have nose for business the same way a journalist has nose for news. A good businessman sees where others don't see.

2. Raising Capital for Startup

After developing an idea, the next challenge that the entrepreneurs are going to face when starting a business from scratch is that of raising capital. An entrepreneur is the only one who knows business idea to the core. Trying to convince investors about something that doesn't exist is definitely a challenge. Trying to make them understand that they are trustworthy and equal to the task is not child's play, especially when building the first business.

There is more to raising capital than just simply asking for money. Majority of the investors want to invest in already established businesses with minimal risk, and they want to be sure that they get returns for the risk they took. Brilliant business ideas never scale through the venture capital stage because the entrepreneur is either not prepared or lacks what it takes to raise the needed capital. To overcome the challenge of raising capital, an entrepreneur must develop the ability to sell their idea and vision to potential investors. In the game of raising capital, an entrepreneur must have a good story to tell, backed by a strong business plan and good persuasion skills.

3. Assembling a Business Team

The third business challenge that an entrepreneur will face in the course of starting a small business from scratch is assembling the right business management team. The process of building a business team starts even before the issue of raising initial start-up capital arises. Most brilliant ideas and products never get funded because the entrepreneur is trying to raise capital as an individual. A business team is a vital, yet often ignored key to raising venture capital successfully.

An entrepreneur is bound to have strengths and weaknesses. That is, the more reason an entrepreneur needs a business team to cover up or compliment their weaknesses. A team is a necessity for building a successful business. It's the duty of an entrepreneur to make sure that their team sees the future as the entrepreneur sees.

They must believe in possibilities and must also be passionate about making that possibility a reality. If they can't grasp the vision, if they can't see the future with business, then they are not worthy being business team. An efficient strategic business team should comprise as a banker, financial adviser, accountant, attorney or legal adviser, and any other specialist that will be of tremendous impact to the business.

4. Finding the Right Business Location

Finding a good business location at the right place is definitely not easy. An efficient location that has a rapidly growing population, good road network, and other amenities at a good place.

5. Finding Good Employees

Most writers and managers crank up the process of finding good employees as an easy task. They define the process of finding an employee as simply presenting the job description and the right employee will surface. Business owners know how difficult it is to find a hardworking, trustworthy employee. Most employees want to work less and get paid more. Finding a good employee who will be passionate about delivering his or her services is quite difficult. Finding good employees is a minor task compared to the business challenge of forging the hired employees into a team. Employees are the representatives to business customers and the outside world. They are a reflection of the business culture and ethics. If an employee is bad or rude to customers, it is going to portray a bad image for the company. So, it must be careful when hiring employees. Remember the golden rule of business; hire slow and fire fast.

6. Finding Good Customers

The sixth challenge an entrepreneur will face in the process of starting a small business from scratch is finding good customers. In the process of building a business, an entrepreneur will come to find out that there are good customers as well as bad customers. Good customers are really hard to find. A good customer will be loyal to the company and will be willing to forgive if the business makes a mistake and apologize. A good customer will try to do the right thing that will benefit both himself and company mutually.

Bad customers will always look for loopholes in the company's policy to exploit and make a few gains. Bad customers will always try to exploit the company's goodwill and look for ways to rip off the company. Bad customers are responsible for bad debts. Good customers build business, and bad customers will always try to liquidate business.

7. Dealing With Competition

Competition is the next challenge an entrepreneur will face when starting a business. Most individuals see competition as a plague but competition as a good challenge. Competition is a benchmark for creativity, the main engine that stimulates innovation and production of quality products at great prices. Without competition, there will be no innovation, and without innovation, the world will be stagnant.

8. Unforeseen Business Challenges and Expenses

Just as a sailor prepares for unexpected storm, just as a pilot is always on the watch for unpredictable bad weather and thunderstorms, so must an entrepreneur be prepared for whatever comes. Unexpected challenges can come in the form of:

- Unexpected law suits
- Inconsistent government policy
- Not being able to make payroll
- Unpaid bills and taxes
- Unexpected resignation of staff
- Bad debts from customers
- Loss of market share
- Dwindling working capital
- Inadequate stock or inventory

These business challenges, if not handled properly, can ruin the plan to build a successful business. Another challenge an entrepreneur must expect is an unforeseen increase in business expenses. If not handled properly, it might result in constant negative cash flow and eventually; business failure.

9. Keeping Up With Industrial Changes and Trends

Change in trends is a challenge an entrepreneur must be prepared for when starting a small business. Trends have made and broken a lot of businesses, profitable businesses that have been wiped out by slight industrial changes and trends. A typical example is the Dot com trend, where many established industrial based businesses were wiped out by new Web-based Dot com companies. Seasoned entrepreneurs know that trend is a friend and are always willing to swiftly adjust their business to the current trend.

10. Exiting the Business

When building a business from scratch, an entrepreneur is going to face the challenge of determining the exit strategy. Most entrepreneurs run their business without any plans to exit, and even if they have an exit strategy, they find it difficult to implement it. Before starting a business, it is advisable to plan an exit. Lack of an exit plan is the primary reason why most businesses crumble after the death of the founder. An exit strategy is very important to the long-term survival of a business. Most smart entrepreneurs will use a certain benchmark as a target, and once this specific target is reached, they exit the business. Examples of such benchmarks are: annual sales, annual turnover, asset base, market saturation, customer base, subscribers, or number of users.

11. Down in the Doldrums

According to several studies, entrepreneurs are more prone to depression and anxiety than the average company employee.

12. Overestimating

Another challenge entrepreneurs face is overestimating their initial success. Company in one year and made millions that you can do the same.

13. Focus

One of the biggest mistakes entrepreneurs make in their early days is trying to be all things to all people. They attempt to sell their product or service to too wide of a market.

Entrepreneurs also face another challenge in this area. They focus on the wrong things. They spend too much time building their product without validating that the marketplace wants needs and will actually pay for it.

14. Passion and Purpose

Many entrepreneurs choose an oxymoronic approach to business. They decide to start their own company because they want unlimited income potential, to be their own boss, and holder of their own destiny. Yet, as they work on building their business, they realize they lack passion for what they are doing.

Suggestions and End Thought

An entrepreneur is one who plays a significant role in the economic development of a country. Basically, an entrepreneur can be regarded as a person who has the initiative, skill, and motivation to set up a business or an enterprise of his or her own and who always looks for high achievement. The most important challenges faced by new entrepreneurs include developing the vision and business idea, raising capital for startup, assembling a business team, finding the right business location, finding good employees, finding good customers, dealing with competition, unforeseen business challenges and expenses, keeping up with industrial changes and trends, lack of support, negative mindset, lack of marketing facilities, lack of infrastructural facilities, and so on. So, it is necessary to overcome these challenges in order to conduct an efficient business.

1. An entrepreneur must possess the ability to see what others cannot see. While others see problems, an entrepreneur must see opportunities.
2. To overcome the challenge of raising capital, an entrepreneur must develop the ability to sell their idea and vision to potential investors.
3. An entrepreneur to make sure that their team sees the future as the entrepreneur see.
4. To find out an efficient location that has a rapidly growing population, good road network, and other amenities at a good place.
5. In order to overcome negative mindset, an entrepreneur should empower himself by reading inspirational articles, successful stories, great books, movies, and so on.
6. In order to overcome lack of support, an entrepreneur should find out a virtual group of people on social media that supports and promotes each other.

About the Authors

Nikhil Agarwal has guided hundreds of entrepreneurs during his career spanning two decades. He helped in raising millions of dollars for his startups. He currently manages the largest incubator of India at IIT Kanpur. He has the additional responsibility of being the CEO of Artificial Intelligence Centre for Excellence, IIT Kanpur. Dr. Agarwal is the Senior Senator of the World Business Angel Forum (WBAF) for India. He was the Pioneer Member and Ambassador—South Asia and Middle East of World Entrepreneurship Forum (WEF). He is the founder of Entrepreneur Café—a global movement connecting 45,000 entrepreneurs as members in 26 countries. He earned his PhD in Science, Technology, and Innovation Studies (STIS) from the University of Edinburgh and MPhil in Technology Policy from the University of Cambridge in the United Kingdom.

LinkedIn profile: www.linkedin.com/in/drnikhilagarwalindia/

Twitter: www.twitter.com/nikhilagarwal7

Krishiv Agarwal is reading to become an economist. As a young startup enthusiast, he is a keen observer of business and markets in developed countries. He extensively writes on fiction and business-related subjects.

Index

www.ingramcontent.com/pod-product-compliance
Lightning Source LLC
Chambersburg PA
CBHW061306220326
41599CB00026B/4762